IMAGES OF THE CITY OF LONDON

The Square Mile Revealed

Warren Grynberg

For Marilyn, Darren and Sara

breedon **books** PUBLISHING

First published in Great Britain in 2005 by

The Breedon Books Publishing Company Limited

Breedon House, 3 The Parker Centre, Derby, DE21 4SZ.

Revised 2009.

Front cover: *Cheapside 1920s, looking east.*

ISBN 978-1-85983-749-8

Printed and bound by TJ International Ltd, Padstow, Cornwall.

Contents

Acknowledgements

The first edition of this book would not have been possible without the valuable help and assistance of the staff of the Guildhall Library, Corporation of London. Roger Appleby, Curator and archivist, City of London Police Museum, Dr Tom Wareham, Curator of the Museum in Docklands, David McCarthy, City of London Cemetery and Crematorium. I am indebted to Trevor Walford, Judges Postcards Ltd, for permission to reproduce the images from the Judges' London series of postcards shown in this book, and finally a thank you to my dear friend Sid Freedman for his help and advice.

Books consulted include:
The London Encyclopaedia edited by Ben Weinreb and Christopher Hibbert.
Dictionary of City of London Street Names by Al Smith.
Images of England: The City of London compiled by Brian Girling.
The Criminal Prisons of London by Henry Mayhew and John Binny.
Prisons and Punishments of London by Richard Byrne.
The City of London by Mary Cathcart Borer.

I thank the following for permission to reproduce images that are their copyright.
(A) Corporation of London.
(B) Commissioner of Police for the City of London.
(C) Judges Postcards of Hastings.
(D) Billingsgate Market, Corporation of London.
(E) London Daily Mail (Solo Syndication).
(F) The Times Newspaper.
(G) Museum of London.
(H) David McCombie.
(I) Lowewood Museum, Borough of Broxbourne.
Map of the City of the City of London by kind permission of Cook, Hammond & Kell Ltd.
All other images are the copyright of the author.

Introduction

If you walk around the City of London, you will find a world class, high-tech business city, one of the world's most important financial centres... but it wasn't always like that.

The history of London goes back 2,000 years to when the Romans invaded Britain. They stayed for 400 years and in that time established London as a military outpost and trading settlement. They built a defensive wall, enclosing approximately one square mile, around their new city. This enclosed area was to become the City of London, known as The Square Mile.

London grew and became an important centre of industry and commerce, spreading in all directions, outgrowing its walls and swallowing up rural villages such as Knightsbridge, Charing Cross and Chelsea. During the 19th century, London became a vast metropolis with the ancient City at its centre.

At the turn of the 20th century, over five percent of the world's population lived in cities and one of the most important and prosperous was the City of London. The Roman and mediaeval walls had long since disappeared, but the City was still affectionately called The Square Mile. Many thousands of people lived here, crowded into small houses or rooms above their shops and workshops. By comparison, the merchants, bankers and the affluent resided in fine houses, some of which may still be found hidden in courtyards and cul-de-sacs.

The City of London became the warehouse of the world; ocean-going ships would spill out their cargoes into the warehouses of its docks, then the largest in the world. The City was a busy, thriving place where business was conducted not only during the week but also in the evenings and at weekends.

The bombing raids of World War Two left much of the City charred and ruined. Thousands of national institutions, office buildings, shops, inns and cafés were damaged or destroyed. The streets and houses were laid to waste and the City's inhabitants were made homeless, but, despite the inconvenience, the business institutions worked day and night to keep the wheels of the City turning. St Paul's Cathedral was damaged, but the churches that had been described as the jewels of the City were left as empty shells or reduced to rubble, just as their predecessors had been left after the Great Fire of London, 350 years previously.

Rebuilding work began in the 1950s and 1960s. Archaeologists were given the opportunity to excavate the bombed areas and record London's past. When they had completed their work, construction work began on a new and modern City. The residents slowly crept back, and today the City has a resident population of between 9,000 and 10,000 people who live mainly in the 1960s built Barbican development.

Today The Square Mile is London's financial and business district and is involved in financial matters of all kinds. But despite its modern facets, the City retains many of its ancient traditions. Guildhall, the civic and administrative centre, is one of the largest mediaeval halls in England. A short walk away is Mansion House, built in the 18th century and the official residence of the Lord Mayor of the City of London. Dominating the City is St Paul's Cathedral, in whose crypt is buried Sir Christopher Wren, the cathedral's architect and the rebuilder of London after the Great Fire.

It has been a difficult task to choose the photographs and postcards for this book. Many have not been seen for years and the quality of some is poor. However, I have included some of these because their content is more important than their quality.

This newly revised edition has been published so that I can share a small part of my collection with you, the reader. It is also an attempt to show what it was really like to live, work and play in the greatest city in the world. A city whose buildings, people and way of life remained relatively undisturbed for generations, until World War Two when it was brutally and savagely torn to pieces, and to later reinvent itself as one of the world's most important financial centres.

I have added an additional chapter, *The City of Fred Judge*, into this new edition. I hope that you enjoy the images and captions as much as I enjoyed preparing them for you.

Warren Grynberg, 2009

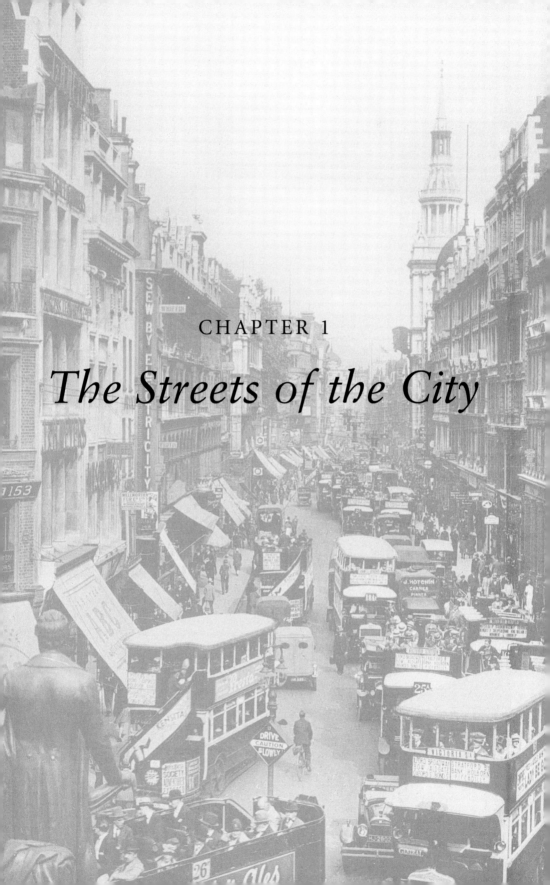

CHAPTER 1

The Streets of the City

Aldgate, c.1920, is at the eastern end of the City and is named after one of the original Roman gates. Aldgate, from the Saxon 'Aelgate', means open to all or free of tolls. The old Roman road to Colchester, Whitechapel, ran east from it. The church steeple is St Botolph's, Aldgate. St Botolph is the patron saint of travellers. So, not surprisingly, many churches with the same dedication were built at city gates to serve as safe havens for travellers. Aldgate East Underground Station, which opened in 1884, is in the foreground.

Bishopsgate, c.1920, was once known as Bishopsgate Street and is one of the longest streets in the City of London. It takes its name from the gate in the city wall where Erkenwald, a Saxon Bishop of London, once lived. Nestling comfortably between the shops, warehouses and offices is the tiny mediaeval church of St Ethelburga-the-Virgin, Bishopsgate. The Roman name for this Street was Ermine Street, which ran from London north to Lincoln and York.

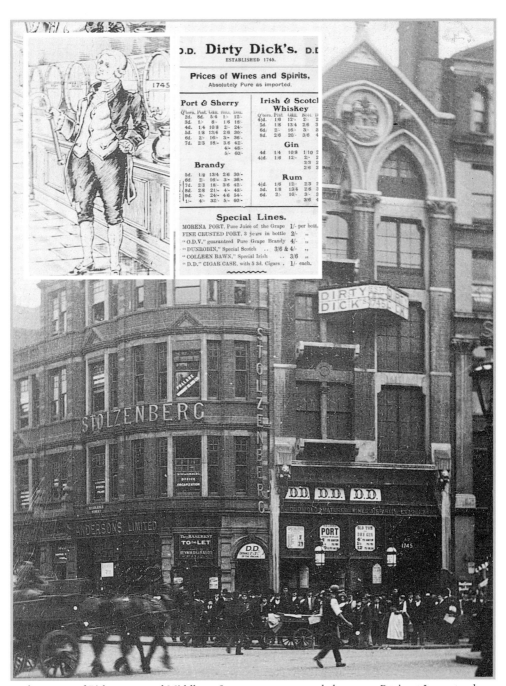

At the corner of Bishopsgate and Middlesex Street, more commonly known as Petticoat Lane, stands Dirty Dick's public house. In 1745 Richard Nathaniel Bentley, a well-to-do dandy, lived in a house on this site. Bentley fell in love with a beautiful girl whom he planned to marry. On the eve of the wedding, after the wedding breakfast had been prepared, he learned that she had died. He was so distraught that he shut himself in the parlour where the celebrations were to be held and lived out the rest of his days in poverty and squalor. The house was demolished and replaced by the pub in 1870.

Bedlam, a hospital founded in 1246 for the sick, and afterwards for the insane, once stood on the site of the Great Eastern Hotel, which can be seen on the right, in Liverpool Street. Liverpool Street Station is just out of sight, but both Broad Street Station, now demolished, and the Metropolitan Railway can clearly be seen. The street has changed very little and some of the buildings in this photograph, taken in 1908, can still be recognised.

The view below is Liverpool Street Station, which opened in 1874. The land for this station was purchased 12 years earlier by the newly formed Great Eastern Railway Company. Originally built with 18 platforms, it was London's largest railway station. Its platforms were built well below street level to comply with City planning regulations.

Busy Cannon Street looking towards St Paul's Cathedral in 1913. Cannon Street was called Candlewick Street in the 13th and 14th centuries because candlemakers lived and worked here. In the forefront of the picture, office workers can be seen waiting for the London showroom and offices of Burroughs Adding Machine Ltd to open.

A view from the steps of the Royal Exchange in 1909. On the left is Mansion House, the official residence of the Lord Mayor of the City of London. To the right is the Bank of England and in the centre is the equestrian statue of the Duke of Wellington. An entrance to Bank Underground Station can be seen in the foreground, with the turret of the now demolished Mappin & Webb building visible beyond.

Threadneedle Street and the Bank of England in the 1920s. The street takes its name from the needles used by the Merchant Taylors' Company, who have their hall at number 30. The Bank retains its 1788 defensive wall, although, within, it was rebuilt and enlarged just before the beginning of World War Two as can be seen in the next photograph.

Looking east towards the Bank of England and Royal Exchange in the late 1930s, this is still the City's busiest road junction, where seven major thoroughfares now converge. The Royal Exchange was founded in 1566 as the first purpose-built trading place in London. Previously, merchants had conducted their business in the streets or in their own homes. Called Gresham's Exchange after its founder, it was renamed the Royal Exchange by Queen Elizabeth I in 1570. Compare this with the previous postcard. Here the Bank of England has been enlarged within its 18th-century walls. The architect was Sir Herbert Baker, and his work was completed in 1937.

Chepe is from a Saxon word meaning bargaining or trading, and hence a market, and Cheapside, seen here in the 1920s, is still a busy street with many shops and bustling crowds. It is also the only street in the City to be narrower now than it used to be in years gone by. Here, too, common criminals were punished in stocks and pillories. A statue of Sir Robert Peel, politician, prime minister and founder of the Metropolitan Police Force in 1839, is to the left of the picture. The statue has been moved to the Metropolitan Police Training College in Hendon, north-west London.

Poultry is the eastern end of Cheapside. The name reminds us of the poulterers who worked and lived here before the Great Fire in 1666. Above the small shops are the fine Victorian façades of commercial institutions. Note the sign depicting 'INCOME TAX RECOVERED', nothing changes. This photograph was taken in 1903.

13

A late afternoon scene in one of the many narrow streets around St Paul's Cathedral, in the 1920s.

The upper postcard shows Staple Inn in Holborn, a rare example of an Elizabethan, 16th century, half-timbered building to have survived the Great Fire of London. In the Middle Ages the staplers, or wool merchants, would bring their wool here to be taxed. The lower card shows the same building in about 1895. Half-timbered buildings were not popular in the 19th century and many were plastered over, but at the end of the century the plaster was removed to reveal the magnificent façades that we can still enjoy today.

St Martin's-le-Grand and the General Post Office in 1905. In the 11th century a monastery was built here. It could provide a safe haven for those who managed to escape from London's prisons on their way to Tyburn (Marble Arch) to be hanged. Those who reached its gates could be given sanctuary, except for traitors who were not allowed to enter. In the 15th century, St Martin's-le-Grand became famous for its lace making and infamous for its counterfeit jewellery.

St Paul's Churchyard, c.1910. The churchyard was a busy thoroughfare with many fine shops and warehouses facing the Cathedral. The Chapter House, built by Sir Christopher Wren after the Great Fire in 1666, is the brick building on the far left. Some of those implicated in the Gunpowder Plot of 1605 were executed in the churchyard.

An atmospheric view of the East Passage that runs parallel to Cloth Fair, close to Smithfield. This narrow, gloomy alleyway is lined with tall, Victorian warehouses, small shops and houses of the poor. It still retains its mediaeval-style gutter that carried not only rainwater but most other types of waste to an inadequate drainage system. The children featured in this early postcard seem to be fascinated by the camera. The street has changed very little since this photograph was taken.

When first flown in 1929, the R101 airship was the largest flying object ever built, at 777ft long. Here she is seen flying gracefully over Fleet Street. This airship was designed to provide luxury air travel throughout the British Empire. On her maiden voyage to India she crashed in bad weather. In the early morning of Saturday 4 October 1930 the huge ship crashed into flames on a hillside near Beauvois in France. Of the 44 people aboard, only six survived. This disaster caused the cancellation of the Airship Scheme that was scrapped the following year.

'The Street of Pen and Ink.' Fleet Street in the 1890s, looking towards Ludgate Circus and St Paul's. Many old buildings on the right side were demolished when the street was widened a few years later. Fleet Street was famous for newspapers, journalists and its literary connections, until the 1980s when the newspaper industry moved to other parts of London.

An early 'Mark V tank bank' slowly trundles its way under the railway bridge at Ludgate Circus in 1918. A novel fund raising scheme, designed to help the war effort during World War One, was implemented in 1918 when tanks were used as gigantic 'money boxes'. The idea was that people would throw their spare change into the tank to raise money for the war against Germany. Those who served in this 29 ton tank were cut-off, with no radio contact or direction from the outside world. It had a crew of eight and conditions inside were unbearable, the heat was intense and the noise deafening from gun and shell fire. Its maximum speed was 4.6mph.

Large crowds gather to watch a 'tank bank' arrive at the Prudential Assurance Company's head office in Holborn Bars, in 1917. Although these bonds paid only 5 percent interest, £25,000,000 was invested by the Pru to help the war effort.

Farringdon Street from Holborn Viaduct, looking south. This street was built in 1737 over the Fleet River, a tributary of the River Thames, because by then the river had become a filthy ditch. The Fleet Prison, a notorious debtors prison, was halfway down on the left, until it was demolished in 1846. The Fleet River now flows below the ground in a pipe to its source in Pond Street, Hampstead, north-west London.

Holborn Viaduct seen from Farringdon Street.

Holborn Viaduct, looking west towards Holborn, in 1911. This, the world's first flyover, was opened by Queen Victoria in 1869 and was built to span the Fleet Valley connecting Newgate Street with Holborn. Previously those wanting to cross the valley did so via the steep Holborn Hill, a dangerous and slippery route, especially during the cold and icy winter months.

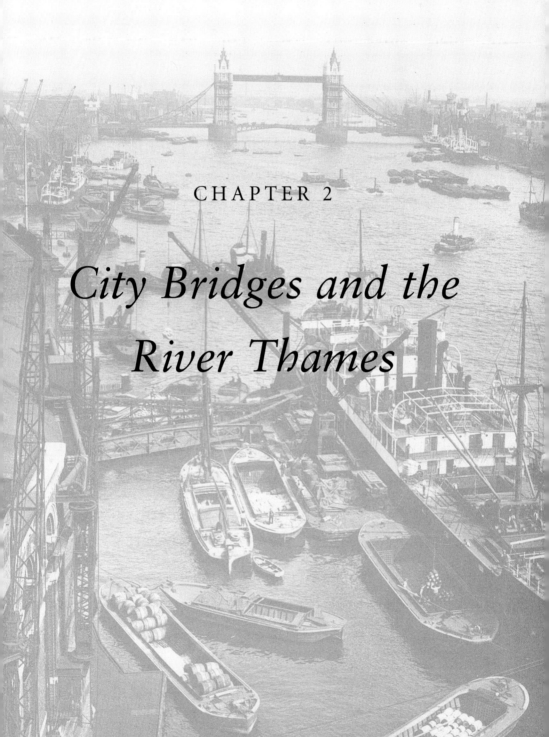

CHAPTER 2

City Bridges and the

River Thames

This photograph, taken from London Bridge, shows the River Thames and the Upper Pool of London, the stretch of river between Tower Bridge and London Bridge, in 1930. Until the demise of London's docks in the mid-1960s, the Pool was a hive of industrial activity. Tugboats would pull ocean-going ships alongside the docks and wharves to unload their cargoes, while barges would constantly be going to and fro along the river.

Tower Bridge on the day it was opened with great ceremony, in 1894, by Edward, Prince of Wales. The bridge was a feat of Victorian engineering and architecture and is one of the City's five bridges over the Thames. Tower Bridge has been raised over one million times to allow shipping to pass into the Upper Pool of London. The Thames Estuary leading to the sea, approximately 50 miles to the east of Tower Bridge, has been London's gateway to Europe since the Romans were here 2,000 years ago.

In 1934, 1,500 tons of sand were dumped on the river bank to create an artificial bathing beach, Tower Beach, in the Pool of London. This picture, taken in the 1950s, shows children at play, with Tower Bridge and the cranes of London's docks in the background. *(G)*

Cross Channel steamers and pleasure craft at Custom House Quay. Ships' masters, merchants and brokers had to report to Custom House, from 1275, to pay customs duty and ensure that the laws regarding the import and export of goods were upheld. The present Custom House dates from 1817 and replaces Sir Christopher Wren's building, which was destroyed by fire.

The original London Bridge, built during the Roman occupation 2,000 years ago, was made from wood. The first stone version of Old London Bridge, left, was built between 1176 and 1215. It was crowded with mediaeval houses, brothels and taverns. This bridge was demolished between 1828 and 1831 and a new bridge opened further upstream, as can be seen in the picture below.

Below: London Bridge in the 1920s. This, the second stone London Bridge, was opened in 1831 to replace the mediaeval bridge that had stood for over 600 years. In the 1960s this bridge was demolished and carefully reconstructed at Lake Havasu, Arizona, and in 1967 a wider and more modern London Bridge was built. In the background is the tower of Southwark Cathedral where Edmund Shakespeare, William's brother, was buried in 1607.

Old London Bridge before its demolition in 1828. The archway, built into the tower of the Church of St Magnus the Martyr, was designed to allow people to walk onto the bridge without stepping into the road. The houses were removed, having become unsafe, in 1758.

These stairs, on the south-west corner of London Bridge, were immortalised by Charles Dickens in *Oliver Twist*. Here, Bill Sykes murdered Nancy in the novel. They are, therefore, known as Nancy's Steps.

A picture of sister paddle-steamers, belonging to the New Palace Steamers Company, the *Royal Sovereign* and *Koh-I-Noor*, meaning 'Mountain of Light' in Indian. They have brought day-trippers to London from the Kent coast and are now starting on the return trip to Ramsgate and Margate. These were the largest and fastest paddlers on the Thames, measuring 300ft from stem to stern. They boasted dining facilities for 200 passengers at one sitting. Other facilities included electric lighting throughout, a post office, ladies' and gentleman's hairdressers, two bathrooms, as well as book and fruit stalls. Cannon Street Station and its railway bridge can be seen in the background.

Southwark Bridge in about 1922, after it had been rebuilt. The first, built between 1814 and 1819, was the largest bridge ever to be made of cast iron. The partially constructed building in the centre of the photograph is the new hall of the Worshipful Company of Vintners, a livery company of the City of London.

The City can be seen in the distance from Southwark. Southwark, too, had its wharves, warehouses, shipping and industry. The centre towers are 'shot towers' where lead shot was manufactured, a trade never practiced in the City. These unique towers, which once lined the river, have all been demolished.

27

Wharves and warehouses overlooked by the dome of St Paul's Cathedral, *c.*1909. The sign for 'Lifebuoy soap' is at Port Sunlight, once the London office of Unilever, then called Lever Brothers. The wharves and warehouse are all gone now, and in their place are modern, high-tech buildings, the new City of London Boys' School and the Millennium Bridge, seen in the photograph below.

The Millennium Bridge, London's first river-crossing in the City for more than a century, was officially opened on 10 June 2001. During this day, and for the next two days, between 80,000 and 100,000 people crossed the new pedestrian bridge and it began rocking and swaying in a frightening manner, leaving walkers clinging on to the sides and people feeling seasick. The bridge was closed two days later and remained closed until 27 February 2002. During that time, modifications were carried out to resolve the problem. The bridge has now been affectionately nicknamed 'the Wobbly Bridge'. The dome of St Paul's Cathedral can be seen in the background, with the City of London Boys' School to the left.

A view of 'The Wobbly Bridge' looking south towards Bankside. The massive brick building with its central chimney is the Tate Modern Art Gallery, converted from a deserted power station.

The Thames Embankment in 1913. To the left of Blackfriars Bridge is the De Keyser's Royal Hotel, established by a Belgian waiter, Polydor de Keyser, in 1874. This luxurious 400-bedroom hotel was much patronised by royalty and nobility from all over Europe, as well as by visitors arriving and departing from Blackfriars Station. Polydor de Keyser acquired British nationality and was elected the first Roman Catholic Lord Mayor of London in 1887. Unilever House, headquarters of Unilever, now stands on the site.

A tram trundles across Blackfriars Bridge on its way to Croydon in south London. Trams were phased out in the early 1950s and the steel rails removed to be sold as scrap. Unilever House, built in 1930, dominates the background.

A battalion of soldiers marches across Blackfriars Bridge towards Southwark during World War One. They are probably on their way to Waterloo Station. The pillars supporting the bridge have been designed to look like pulpits, as a reminder of the Blackfriars Monastery that occupied the area in the Middle Ages. King Henry VIII closed the Monastery in 1538 and demolished the buildings after confiscating its treasures.

The Mermaid Theatre, Puddle Dock, east of Blackfriars Bridge, on the site of a bombed Victorian warehouse. It was the dream of an actor, Sir Bernard Miles, to open the first theatre in the City after a gap of over 300 years. The new theatre was officially opened by the Lord Mayor on 28 May 1959. It is now a conference centre.

The river bank reached the buildings beyond the trees until 1864 when over 35 acres of land was reclaimed from the Thames and a wall built to contain the water. At the same time this new road, the Victoria Embankment, was constructed from Westminster to the City, and below ground a new sewerage system was constructed for London. This photograph was taken from Blackfriars Bridge.

'The Flying Squad', Port of London Authority policemen, in the 1930s, taking part in annual life-saving practice in the London Docks, and at the same time testing out newly-designed kapok filled life jackets. (G)

The Thames at Teddington. Until 1857 the City of London was responsible for the tidal stretch of the river from the Thames Estuary in the east to Teddington Lock, pictured here, 66 miles to the west. The name Teddington is said to have derived from the mediaeval name Tide-End-Town. It appears that in 1197 King Richard I, the Lionheart, gave control of the tidal stretch of the river to the City in return for a large sum of money that he needed to finance a crusade.

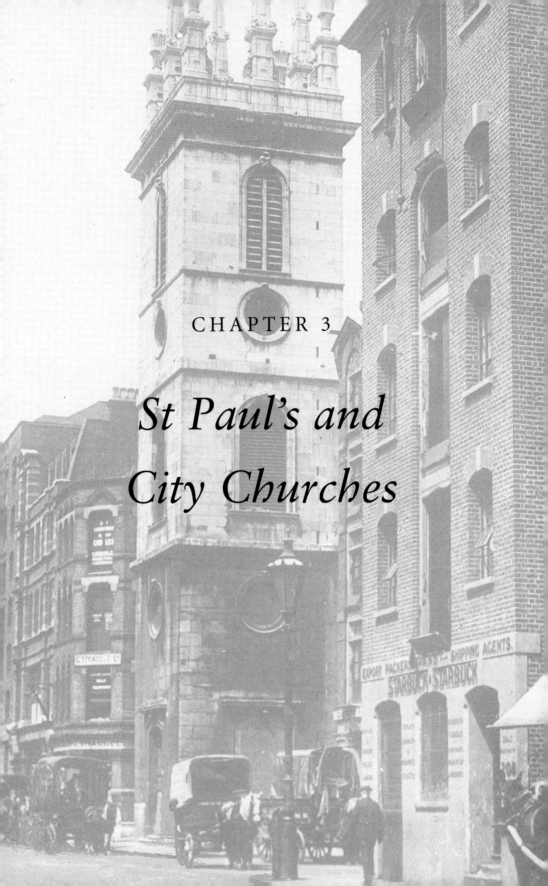

CHAPTER 3

St Paul's and
City Churches

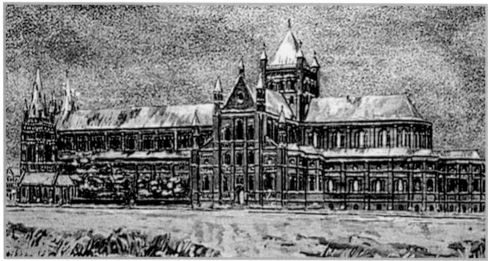

Building work began on the fourth St Paul's cathedral in 1087. It became one of the largest churches in England, considerably larger and higher than today's building. Markets were held in the nave, where people would socialise, and during the wet, winter months it was used as a dry shortcut from Cheapside in the east to Ludgate in the west. In the 17th century, St Paul's was used by Oliver Cromwell's cavalry, who stabled their horses here. Publishers, printers and booksellers stored their books and paper in the crypt for safety. Old St Paul's dominated the City for over 500 years, but on the night of 4 September 1666 it was so severely damaged in the Great Fire of London that it was never rebuilt.

Two early pictures show the western front of the early Norman cathedral, c.1160, and the south facing façade and steeple. The spire, seen in the photograph opposite, was added later.

St Paul's, dedicated to the patron saint of London, is the masterpiece of a man of genius, Britain's most admired architect, Sir Christopher Wren. Wren was not a trained architect but a Professor of Mathematics, a scientist and Fellow of All Soul's College at Oxford University. He had a remarkable gift for designing buildings without any formal training. The early 20th century postcard above shows the present cathedral that took 35 years to complete. It was the world's first purpose-built Protestant church, consecrated in 1710 during the reign of Queen Anne, whose statue is in the forecourt. To celebrate the 300th anniversary of its consecration, the Cathedral embarked on a £50 million restoration programme to see St Paul's repaired and cleaned inside and out. Compare the postcard above to the modern photograph on the left.

35

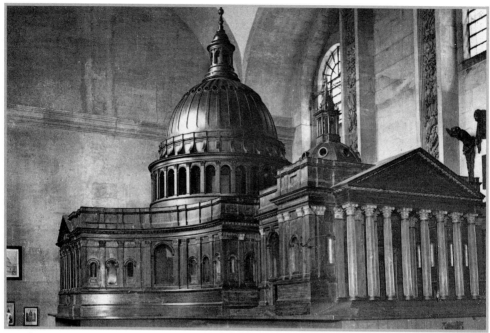

Wren's Great Model, made in 1674; not the church he eventually built but the one he wanted to build. The designs were rejected by the Dean and Chapter, as well as by King Charles II. Beautifully made with great attention to detail, the Great Model, measuring 20ft long, has been restored and is displayed in the library.

The statue of Queen Anne, who ascended the throne in 1702 and died in 1714, dominates the west front. It was during her reign that the new Cathedral was consecrated. As she has her back to the cathedral, a contemporary satirist wrote, referring to her drinking habits: 'Brandy Nan, Brandy Nan, you've been left in the lurch, your face to the gin shop with your back to the church'. Two of the allegorical figures surrounding the statue represent France and America. The Stuart monarchs recognised France as English territory, and America was still under British rule in 1710.

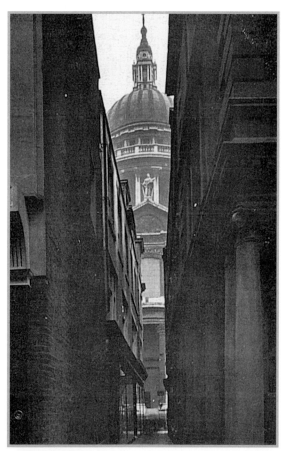

An atmospheric view of the dome and north transept from Canon Alley, off Paternoster Row. The tiny streets and alleyways around St Paul's were swept away during the Blitz of World War Two. Gustav Doré, the celebrated 19th-century illustrator, said that, '*this was the finest view of the Cathedral*'.

The Geometrical Staircase in the south-west tower of the Cathedral. This remarkable 17th century staircase has 92 steps but no visible means of support. Each step is fixed only inches into the wall and yet is able to support the one above. The balustrade is the work of Jean Tijou, an 18th-century, French ironworker. Tijou was also responsible for the designs of the screens and grilles.

A 1913 survey revealed that much of the 17th-century stonework was in urgent need of repair. Restoration work started immediately: scaffolding was erected and liquid cement pumped into the piers to strengthen them. At the same time, broken masonry was replaced and a steel chain was fitted around the dome.

Looking east towards the Victorian high altar, on either side are the original furnishings that date from 1695–7. These exquisitely decorated choir stalls were carved by the Anglo-Dutch sculptor and woodcarver Grinling Gibbons. The grand 19th century high altar stands at the east end. It was installed in 1888 to replace the original, a simple wooden table belonging to Wren, all that could be afforded at the time. The cost of Wren's new cathedral was in excess of £72,000,000, the equivalent of many hundreds of millions of pounds today.

The effigy of John Donne, poet, preacher and Dean of St Paul's between 1621 and 1634. This monument, which shows Donne wearing the grave-cloth in which he was to be buried, is the only complete figure from Old St Paul's to have survived the Great Fire of London. Scorch marks from the fire can be seen on the urn. The sculptor, Nicholas Stone, was paid £160 for his work, then a very large sum of money. *(C)* (©*Judges Postcards Ltd, Hastings*)

Sir Christopher Wren, mathematician and astronomer as well as architect of genius, died, aged 91 years, in 1723. He was buried in a quiet corner in the crypt of his Cathedral. His epitaph, translated from Latin, reads: '*Beneath lies buried the founder of this Church and City, Christopher Wren, who lived more than ninety years not for himself but for the public good. Reader, if you seek his monument, look around you*'.

Above is the Church of St Ethelburga-the-Virgin within Bishopsgate. This, the smallest church in London, was dedicated to St Ethelburga, the daughter of Ethelbert, the first Christian king of Kent in the sixth century. The small shop in front of the church dates from the 1570s. The last owner was Mr Robinson, a spectacle maker. Each Sunday, before services, Mr Robinson opened up his spectacle shop to allow the congregation access to the church behind. In 1933 the shop was pulled down in order to widen the pavement.

Below, a peep through Mr Robinson's spectacle shop into St Ethelburga's. The church was tiny, and it measured only 51ft long and less than 30ft wide. In the 1860s it became known for its Anglo-Catholic liturgy, hence the rare rood-screen seen in the postcard. It achieved notoriety in the 1930s and 1940s as one of the few London churches in which divorced people could remarry. Unlike many of the City churches, St Ethelburga's was unscathed during the Great Fire of London and the Blitz of World War Two. However, on Saturday 24 April 1993, a massive IRA bomb exploded opposite, destroying the church and surrounding area. After eventually being rebuilt, on 12 November 2002 St Ethelburga's was reconsecrated. The following day, the St Ethelburga's Centre for Peace and Reconciliation was officially opened by HRH the Prince of Wales.

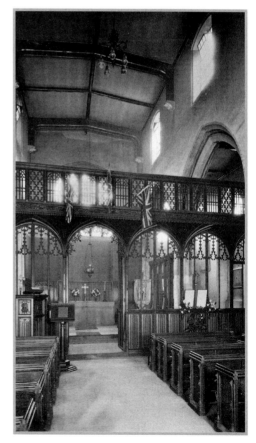

The destruction to St Ethelburga's caused by the 1993 IRA bomb, and the newly built church blending with the hi-tech and modern Swiss Re headquarters, proving that the new can live happily with the old.

St Bartholomew-the-Great, Smithfield, was founded in 1123 by Rahere, a courtier of King Henry I. Beyond the graveyard are 17th century houses, untouched by the Great Fire. St Bartholomew Hospital is next to the church and was founded at the same time.

Inside St Bartholomew-the-Great. The founder's tomb, close to the altar, has been protected with sandbags during Zeppelin bombing raids in 1915, during World War One.

Above: the Church of the Austin Friars. There was an Augustinian monastery here, from 1253, until King Henry VIII closed it in the 16th century. His son, King Edward VI, later gave the nave as a gift to Dutch refugees, and it has remained London's only Dutch church ever since. The church was rebuilt in the 1950s after being badly damaged during World War Two.

Left: St Bride's, Fleet Street, dedicated to St Bridget, an Irish saint. It is famous for its wedding cake steeple, as well as for being the journalist's church. Roman, Saxon and mediaeval remains uncovered by the bombing of World War Two, including an unusual iron coffin, are on display in the crypt. It was said that a pastry-maker living nearby was so inspired by Sir Christopher Wren's design of the steeple that he made the first tiered wedding cake. The bride for whom the cake was made presented her wedding dress to the church as a gift. It is displayed in a glass-case at the bottom of the stairs leading into the crypt.

43

St Mary-the-Virgin, Aldermanbury, was badly damaged during an air raid in December 1940. After the war the remaining masonry was sent to Westminster College, Foulton, Missouri, in the US, where the church was rebuilt to Wren's original designs as a tribute to Sir Winston Churchill. An attractive garden now covers the site. There is a memorial to John Heminge and Henry Condell, who are buried here. These two actor friends of William Shakespeare first published his plays in 1623, known as 'Shakespeare's First Folio'.

St Dunstan's-in-the-East, Eastcheap. Today all that remains is its shell, around which a garden has been created. The tower and steeple are said to have been designed by Wren's daughter, Jane. During a hurricane that swept London in 1703, Wren was told that every steeple had either been damaged or destroyed. Wren's curt reply was: *'Not St Dunstan's, I am sure'*. St Dunstan's was heavily damaged during the Blitz so was never rebuilt. It is now a peaceful garden and open to the public.

This church tower is the only one in London to be built by the Puritans, during the Commonwealth, All Hallows, Barking-by-the-Tower. There has been a church on this site since the seventh century. A Saxon arch was revealed after bomb damage during World War Two. In 1644 Mr and Mrs William Penn brought their baby son to be baptised here. His name was also William and he became the founder of Pennsylvania. John Quincy Adams, later the sixth President of the United States of America, was married here in 1697.

All that remains today of St Mary's, Somerset, is a lonely tower on a traffic island in Upper Thames Street. At the turn of the 20th century, this street was much narrower and the church stood alongside the warehouses. The main body of the church was demolished following an Act of Parliament in 1872. The warehouse, in the forefront, belongs to the shipping agent Starbuck & Starbuck. Could they have shipped coffee to London?

The late mediaeval church of St Olave, Hart Street, was immortalised by Charles Dickens as 'The Church of St Ghastly Grim', a reference to the skull and crossbones above the entrance to the graveyard. Samuel Pepys, the 17th century diarist, lived across the street and St Olave's was his parish church. He lies buried, alongside his wife, beneath the altar. The noticeboard is a reminder that 365 plague victims were buried here, including the legendary Mother Goose, who was buried here in 1586.

The Church of St Sepulchre-without-Newgate, Holborn Viaduct, c.1905. In the 12th century the Crusaders started their journeys to the Holy Land from here so they named this church after the Holy Sepulchre in Jerusalem. Captain John Smith, the 17th-century explorer who founded Jamestown, Virginia, is buried here. The ashes of Sir Henry Wood, founder of the 'Proms', are interred in the Musician's Chapel, and Dame Nellie Melba, the opera singer for whom the peach melba was created, is commemorated in this, the City's largest church.

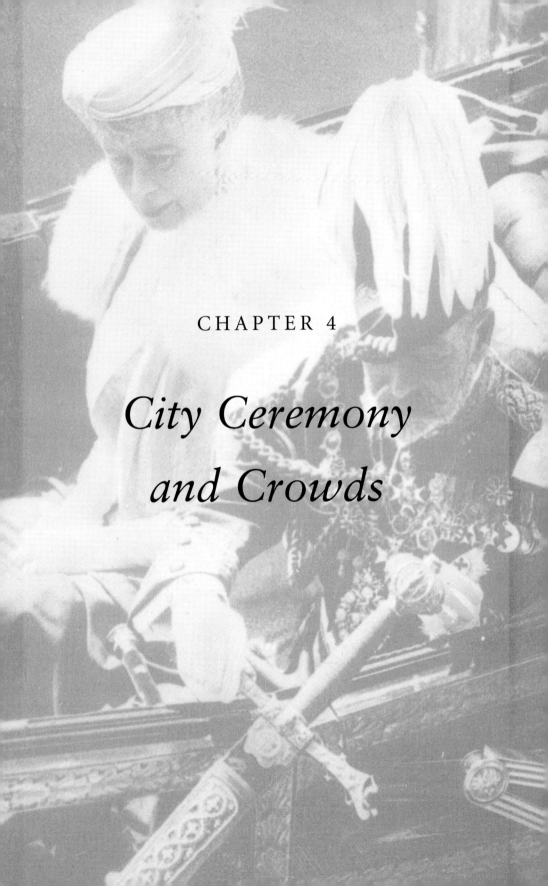

CHAPTER 4

City Ceremony
and Crowds

Crowds throng Petticoat Lane market on a busy Sunday morning in 1913. Situated at the eastern edge of the City, close to the London's East End, this was predominantly a Jewish market. It was so named after the petticoats and second-hand clothes once sold here by poor Jewish peddlers. Religious laws forbade Jews to work on a Saturday, so special dispensation from the authorities allowed the market to open on Sunday mornings instead. The street has been renamed Middlesex Street and the market, the largest in London, continues to operate on Sunday mornings

The Lord Mayor's coach in the Coronation procession of King Edward VII in 1902. The coach was built in 1757 at a cost of £860. Until the early 1950s, it had no brakes and relied on the expertise of the coachman to bring it to a halt. It is permanently on display in the Museum of London and brought out each year for the Lord Mayor's Show.

Temple Bar in Fleet Street, decorated for the coronation of King George V and Queen Mary in 1911. City gentlemen wearing their fashionable 'straw boaters' are walking past the Royal Courts of Justice on the left. A horse-drawn van belonging to Thorleys the poulterer is busy making deliveries to local pubs and restaurants. Temple Bar marks the City of London's western boundary.

The Bank of England is illuminated to
celebrate King George V's and Queen
Mary's coronation, which took place in
Westminster Abbey on 22 June 1911. This
was one of the first occasions in London
where electric light bulbs were used to
decorate a building, and across the street
the Royal Exchange is decorated with
bunting for the occasion as seen in the
photograph on the right.

Armistice Day is observed at the Mansion House on 11 November 1918. As the 11th hour of the 11th day of the 11th month approached, the guns that deafened Europe during World War One stopped firing. Over 10,000,000 people had died, and, as the bells of St Paul's rang out at 11am, hundreds of thousands of Londoners observed a two-minute silence in honour of them. Crowds are gathered outside the Lord Mayor's official residence, Mansion House, for this solemn event.

The funeral procession of nurse Edith Cavell, whose body was exhumed and brought back from Belgium in 1919. Nurse Cavell was executed by the Germans for hiding Allied soldiers and helping them to escape capture during World War One. Her funeral service was held at Westminster Abbey, and thousands of people paid tribute as her funeral cortège, escorted by military and Salvation Army bands, reached Bank Junction on its final journey to Liverpool Street Station; from there her coffin was taken to Norwich Cathedral for burial on 15 May 1919.

An armed military guard arrives at the Bank of England. The tradition of putting the Bank under military protection each night originated from when it was attacked during the Gordon Riots of 1780. This custom continued until 1973 when the Bank's own security force took over.

Election Day at Guildhall in 1906. Members of the City Livery companies, dignitaries and the outgoing Lord Mayor are entering their 'wickets' to nominate the short-list of candidates from which the new Lord Mayor would be chosen. This election takes place each year on 29 September, Michaelmas Day.

King George V and Queen Mary leaving St Paul's Cathedral on 7 July 1929 after attending a thanksgiving service for the King's recovery from illness. The King had suffered from an abscess which caused blood poisoning, but his life had been saved by major surgery.

Queen Victoria Street at its junction with the Embankment and Blackfriars Bridge. Union flags and City flags wave gently in the breeze to welcome their Majesties on their Jubilee day. In the background is Unilever House, and the Black Friar public house is tucked away on the right.

The Lord Mayor's coach after its arrival at the Royal Courts of Justice in the Strand during a Lord Mayor's Show. It is here that the newly elected Lord Mayor takes his oath of allegiance to the Crown before the Judges of the Queen's Bench.

The newly elected Lord Mayor of the City of London in 1930, Sir William Phene Neil, leaving the Royal Courts of Justice during the Lord Mayor's Show. Standing next to him is the outgoing Lord Mayor, the City Sword Bearer, other dignitaries and, at the far right, the Sergeant-at-Arms, holding the Mace, whose attention seems to be distracted. *(A)*

The newly elected Lord Mayor of the City of London in 2008, showing himself to the citizens during the Lord Mayor's Show, protected by his traditional bodyguard, the Pikemen of the Honorary Artillery Company. St Paul's Cathedral is in the background. *(A)*

The Lord Mayor arrives back at Mansion House after the 1955 Lord Mayor's Show. For the first time, the coach was drawn by six of Whitbread Brewery's dappled-grey shire horses, driven and escorted by eight of their draymen. Whitbread's famous brewery has been established in the City of London, in Chiswell Street and Ropemaker Street, for over 270 years.

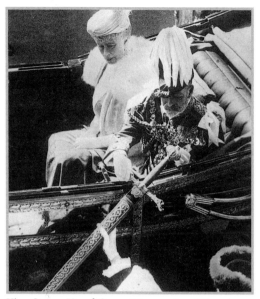

King George V and Queen Mary arrive at Temple Bar on the occasion of their Silver Jubilee on 6 May 1935. The Lord Mayor is offering the City sword to the King as a sign of the City's loyalty. The King touches the handle and then returns it and the sword is carried at the head of the procession to demonstrate that the Monarch is under the Lord Mayor's protection when in the City.

Brilliant sunlight shines into St Paul's during King George V and Queen Mary's Silver Jubilee service. The nave is packed with guests from all over the world.

Queen Mary with King George V at prayer. They were married on 6 July 1893. Queen Mary had been previously engaged to George's elder brother, Prince Edward Albert, Duke of Clarence, who died of pneumonia in 1892.

The dome of St Paul's, floodlit on the night of the Jubilee celebrations. This photograph was taken on Ludgate Hill, which is decorated with bunting and flags.

Crowds rushing to board the No. 15 bus at Ludgate Hill on their way home from work in the early 1930s. The number of the bus tells us that the passengers probably live, or are going shopping, in the posh West End of London as the direction of the bus is shown as Marble Arch.

Crowds gather outside the Royal Exchange to gape at the 'Cornhill Crash'. Shortly before midnight on Saturday 6 August 1927, a large section of the Commercial Union Assurance building collapsed into an adjacent building site. Work on the foundations of the new head office of Lloyds Bank was suspended. The next morning, as a result of the subsidence, a wide crack appeared in the road causing Cornhill and the surrounding streets to be closed for several weeks, resulting in severe traffic chaos.

On Ascension Day a parish beadle and City policeman, wearing their traditional uniforms, lead a procession to 'Beat the Bounds', an ancient ceremony that confirms the boundary marks of the parish. They are followed by parishioners, parish clerks and clergy who beat the boundary with willow wands. Cloth-capped gentlemen amusingly follow the procession from the pavement. Today the boundaries are marked with metal studs in the ground.

St Bartholomew's Hospital in 1939. Every Wednesday afternoon crowds of people assembled at the King Henry VIII gate in Smithfield to see their friends and relatives on the only day that hospital visits were allowed. The barrow on the right is selling fruit and flowers for the patients. The hospital was founded in 1123 and is the oldest one in England still on its original site. The appeal banner hanging above the gate proudly boasts that the hospital has never closed since 1123. Sir William Wallace, the Scottish patriot known as Braveheart, was executed nearby in 1305.

Pearly Kings and Queens on their way into the City to take part in a charity event, possibly at Guildhall. They were market traders, mainly selling fruit and vegetables. Their tradition started in Victorian times and Pearly Kings and Queens still reign today in some parts of London. Their magnificent suits, hats and dresses are adorned with mystic symbols such as stars, moons, flowers and diamonds. Each outfit can have as many as 30,000 buttons individually sewn on and can weigh as much as 60 to 70lbs. These suits are worn at pageants, charity events, christenings, weddings and funerals.

Escape artists, bound heavily with chains and locked into sacks, entertain crowds. Sometimes swords would be entwined with the chains to make escape more difficult. Vast crowds would watch this daring spectacle at Tower Hill as well as in other parts of London such as Charing Cross and Trafalgar Square.

Aldgate, the eastern boundary of the City, in 1935. Jubilee decorations have been strung across this busy street at its junction with the Minories. The banner shows that Aldgate is in Portsoken ward, one of the 26 wards or administrative areas of the City.

CHAPTER 5

The Vanished City

The Mappin & Webb building stood at the junction of Queen Victoria Street and Poultry. It was an impressive example of Victorian Gothic architecture and was built in 1870. The company was originally established in 1774, and in 1897 were granted Royal Warrants as silversmiths to HM the Queen and the Prince of Wales. It was unfortunate that this landmark was demolished in 1994 to make way for a post-modern building, No. 1 Poultry, featured in the modern photograph below. The new building provides office space, restaurants and shops. The redevelopment programme unearthed much archaeological evidence to prove that Poultry and Cheapside were Roman London's main thoroughfares, 2,000 years ago.

Guildhall, c.1910, has been the administrative and civic heart of the City since 1411 when the Great Hall was built. It is the only building in the picture that survives. The building to the right housed the Corporation of London's art collection. A new gallery was opened here in 1999, and London's lost Roman amphitheatre was discovered 18ft below street level during excavations. Opposite was the 18th century Guildhall Justice Room, demolished in 1972 to make way for the new bookshop, library and clock museum. The memorial fountain, erected in 1866, was dismantled at the same time.

Busy Broad Street Station in 1906. This mansion-like building was the City terminus of the North London Railway Company. In its heyday it was London's third busiest station, but by the time it was closed in 1984 it was almost derelict and deserted.

Ludgate Hill at the turn of the 20th century. This was London's traditional processional route between the City and Westminster. The cast-iron bridge carried steam trains to both Ludgate Hill Station and Farringdon Station further north. The trains of the Thameslink Line were diverted to run below ground when the bridge was dismantled in 1990 as part of the new Ludgate development plan. Beyond the bridge can be seen the sleek spire belonging to the Church of St Martin, Ludgate, and the dome of St Paul's. The Lud Gate, like the other City gates, were demolished in the 1750s.

The *Daily Express* Building, Fleet Street, in the 1930s. This unique art deco building, opened in 1932, was faced with black glass and was one of London's first to have a glass-curtain wall. A lorry bearing rolls of heavy newsprint stands ready to be unloaded. In common with the other national newspapers published here, millions of copies were printed each night in the vast basements below the street. Today the newspapers, journalists and printers have all but vanished from Fleet Street. The *Daily Express* Building, now used for other purposes, remains as a monument to a newspaper industry now moved from this 'Street of Pen and Ink'.

Fore Street, Cripplegate, in 1900. Workshops, small factories and houses once occupied this industrial part of the City. On 25 August 1940 the first bomb of World War Two fell on the City, destroying Fore Street and the surrounding area, including the archway leading to the ancient Church of St Giles', Cripplegate. A factory belonging to HB Bentley occupied rooms above the archway. They were manufacturers of high-quality scarves and ties worn by City businessmen. Today Fore Street is part of the Barbican development, built in the early 1960s to replace over 36 acres destroyed in the Blitz. (See Chapter 10)

This old tavern stood in Bishopsgate until 1890 when it was swept away in the early redevelopment of Liverpool Street Station. It had been the home of Sir Paul Pindar, a 17th century merchant who was an Ambassador to Turkey. Sir Paul was financially ruined after lending large sums of money to King Charles II that was never repaid. The preserved façade of his house is displayed in the Victoria and Albert Museum in Kensington, south-west London.

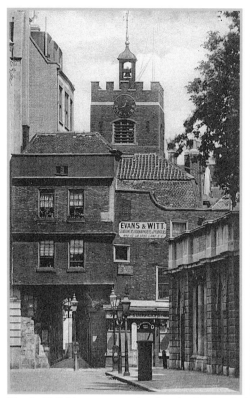

The Smithfield entrance to the church of St Bartholomew-the-Great. A timber-framed house was built above the entrance in the 16th century. Because Elizabethan architecture was not popular during the Victorian period, the original façade was bricked over. In 1915 a bomb fell nearby revealing the Tudor façade, which can also be seen in the postcard on the right. *(C)* (*©Judges Postcards Ltd, Hastings*)

The City Terminus Hotel, later renamed the Cannon Street Hotel, was established in 1867 and was built in front of Cannon Street Railway Station. The Communist Party of Great Britain was founded here in 1920. The hotel closed in 1931 and the rooms were converted into offices. The hotel was demolished after World War Two and the area was redeveloped in 1965.

Ye Olde Dick (Whittington) in Cloth Fair was probably London's oldest tavern, dating from the 15th century. Sir Richard (Dick) Whittington, after whom the tavern was named, is often portrayed as a pantomime character. In reality he was a wealthy City merchant and philanthropist who was elected Lord Mayor of London four times during the 15th century. Cloth Fair is named after the cloth market that was held in the street. Ben Jonson, author of *Bartholomew Fair*, lived near here. Ye Olde Dick Whittington was demolished in 1916.

The City of London Lying-In Hospital in City Road was an austere Victorian building near the junction of Old Street and City Road. This maternity hospital relied heavily on charity and was established in 1750 within the City, but later it was moved to a site just outside its boundaries. It was intended to be used by poor, married women, women expecting difficult births and those who lived in unsanitary conditions. The name was changed to the City of London Maternity Hospital when it moved to Hertfordshire in the 1950s. The hospital finally closed in 1983.

The oldest building in Cheapside was on the corner of Friday Street. This remarkable building withstood the Great Fire of 1666 and served as the City branch of Meakers the Gentlemens' Outfitter until it was demolished in 1956. In mediaeval times Cheapside was known as 'The Chepe' from a Saxon word meaning marketplace or bargain.

LONDON'S SMALLEST SHOP.

"Daily Graphic"]   [Photograph.

London's smallest shop in 1900, measuring barely five feet by four feet (152cm x 122cm), at an entrance to Bank Underground Station on the City and South London Railway, now part of the Northern Line. Mr Blanchard, a tobacconist and the owner, can be seen chatting to a customer, in what was probably London's first kiosk.

Christ's Hospital, Newgate Street. Four views, dating from 1903. Founded in 1553 by King Edward VI and originally built as a hospital for orphans, it occupied the buildings of the Greyfriars Monastery, dissolved during the Reformation 30 years earlier. The boys wore a distinctive uniform, comprising a long blue coat and bright yellow stockings. It was said that the colour chosen for the stockings kept the rats away from the boys' ankles. The orphanage eventually became a grammar school and in 1902 it moved to Horsham in Sussex. The original buildings were demolished to make way for new extensions to the General Post Office in King Edward Street. The boys still wear their blue coats, and, the school is known as the Blue Coat School.

Boys on parade standing in front of the main building. The tower on the left is St Sepulchre's Church in Newgate Street.

Pupils relax and read while a nurse attends one of the sick boys in the school's infirmary.

The main entrance in Newgate Street. Students pose with the school's doorman for a photograph. Above the arch is a statue of the founder, King Edward VI, the only son of Henry VIII.

Boys wearing their long frock coats learn to play hockey at the entrance to the parade ground.

An atmospheric view of how Cloth Fair used to be in 1900. The narrow lanes, tiny shops and stucco-faced exteriors have disappeared to make way for modern redevelopment and housing.

Temple Bar, the old western gate into the City, was designed by Sir Christopher Wren in 1670 and stood where Fleet Street meets The Strand. The heads and gory body parts of executed traitors were displayed on its spikes. Temple Bar was dismantled in 1878 because it caused major traffic congestion. It lay in pieces in a railway yard for 10 years until it was purchased by Sir Henry Bruce Meux, a wealthy brewery owner, as a birthday gift for his wife. In its place, the Temple Bar Memorial was set up in 1880. The monument, a tall pedestal surmounted by a griffin, stands on a traffic island in the middle of the road. Here the Lord Mayor of the City of London offers the City sword to the Monarch before entering the City, a sign of the City's loyalty.

The old gate, comprising more than 2,000 stones weighing over 350 tons, was carefully transported from London to Hertfordshire and re-erected as the main entrance into the Meux family estate in Theobalds Park. The room above the gate was regularly used to hold dinner parties. Among those invited were Mr Winston Churchill, King Edward VIII and other royalty, politicians and guests.

Temple Bar fell into disrepair and became dilapidated. In 1976 it was entrusted to the Temple Bar Trust charity, which aimed to return it to the City where it once belonged. In 2001 the Corporation of London, the local government of the City of London, along with other City donors, agreed to fund the project to the sum of £3,000,000.

On 10 November 2004, three years later, Temple Bar, rebuilt as Wren would have seen it, was officially opened by the Lord Mayor. Today it is the elegant gateway connecting St Paul's Cathedral with the modern, recently redeveloped, Paternoster Square. These images are of Temple Bar during its turbulent history, spanning more than three centuries.

Temple Bar and the City's western boundary. This busy view, c.1870, looks east from The Strand towards Fleet Street.

A lonely policeman stands by Temple Bar prior to its removal in 1878. Construction work had already begun on the new Royal Courts of Justice, The Law Courts, in the Strand, and the scaffolding is on the right. *(A)*

This rare and atmospheric photograph is of Lady Meux standing casually at the half-opened gate. *(A)*

Temple Bar became dilapidated and fell into disrepair when Theobalds House ceased to have any residents. Standing sorrowfully amid black garbage sacks with an abandoned car nearby, it was fenced off to prevent vandalism. *(A)*

The Temple Bar
Memorial in the 1920s
looking east towards
Fleet Street.

Sir Henry Meux, heir to the well-known London brewery, relaxing with his wife Lady Valerie, a banjo playing barmaid and former chorus girl. Forever trying to convince Victorian high society of her respectability, she decided to rebuild Temple Bar as the grand entrance to her Hertfordshire estate.

She was never considered the right 'type' to marry Sir Henry. The stories concerning her outrageous activities are many. On one occasion having quarrelled with the vicar she tied her pet tiger to the front of the house to prevent him from entering.

Lady Meux died in 1910 leaving her collection of Ethiopian and Eqyptian antiquities to the British Museum, who refused them. The collection was later sold at auction (I).

A detail of the Temple Bar Memorial. City police officers are chatting to a party of visitors, while a man peeps out from behind the gas lamp wearing his fashionable coke or bowler hat. (A)

On 10 November 2004 the Lord Mayor officially returned Temple Bar to the City of London. Accompanied by the Sheriffs and City officials, he unveiled a plaque before officially pushing open its gates, weighing just over 1.2 tons each, helped by 14 of the stone masons who had worked on the project.

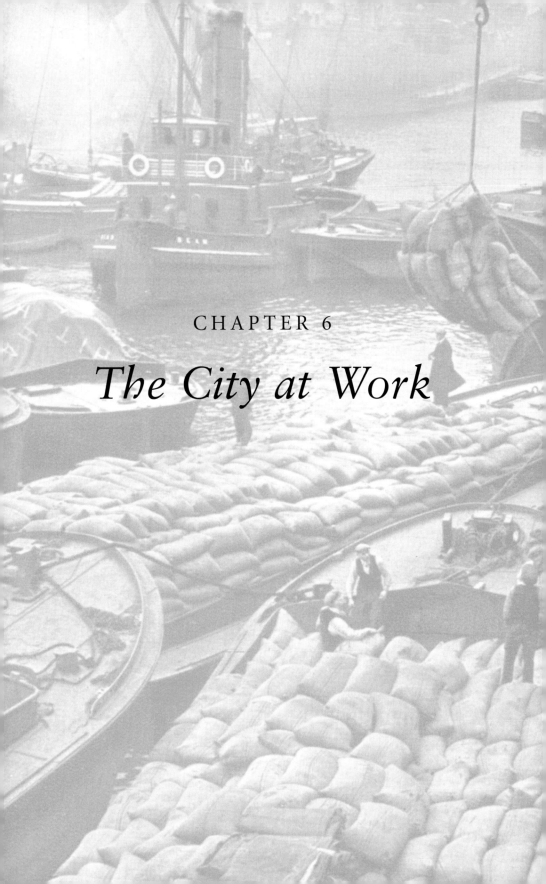

CHAPTER 6

The City at Work

Rush hour around the Royal Exchange, *c.*1908. Each weekday morning thousands of City workers hurry to their offices on foot or by horse-drawn omnibus, while the traders and costermongers saunter along in their horse-drawn carts. The old Bank of England, on the left, was rebuilt in the 1930s. The Bank is nicknamed 'The Old Lady of Threadneedle Street' as a reminder of the seamstresses who once worked in the area. In 1916 the Bank purchased the defunct St Luke's lunatic asylum in Old Street. The hospital was converted into a printing works for the production of banknotes, which were printed there for over 30 years. In the early 1950s the printworks moved to a new purpose-built site in Essex, 14 miles from the City of London. The postcard below, postmarked 1902, shows the first print works at the beginning of the 20th century. Then, postcards mailed to local addresses in the morning were usually delivered later the same afternoon.

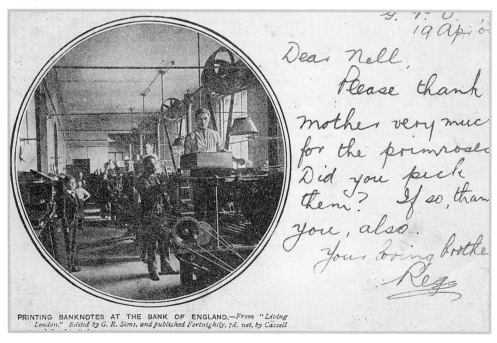

PRINTING BANKNOTES AT THE BANK OF ENGLAND.—*From "Living London." Edited by G. R. Sims, and published Fortnightly, 7d. net, by Cassell*

Businessmen in top hats pose for the camera with the counter-clerks in the 18th century banking hall. This postcard is dated 1904.

A City gent wearing his fashionable bowler, purchasing a ticket at Bank Underground Station at the turn of the 20th century. The Central Railway Company, who operated their trains on the Central Line, adopted a flat fare of 2d, attracting the friendly nickname 'The Twopenny Tube'. Here police officers stand to attention for the camera alongside a tube operator and flat-capped gentleman in the ticket hall.

Waiting on the wooden-slatted platform for a Central Line train on the 'Twopenny Tube' at Bank Station in 1903. Note the advertisement for Nestlé, a Swiss company that still manufactures dairy products and chocolate.

Smithfield Meat Market in 1905. There has been a cattle and meat market on the Smooth Field (Smithfield) as far back as the 12th century. Smithfield opens for business at 5am on weekdays, and by early afternoon, when the day's trading has ended, only the bookkeepers are left to tot up the takings.

A grand view of Smithfield Meat Market. This, the largest wholesale meat market in England, dates from 1868 and was built by Sir Horace Jones, the City's architect, who also built Billingsgate and Leadenhall Markets. Butchers with their horse-drawn wagons crowd the surrounding streets waiting to take away their purchases. Meat, in one form or another, has been cut up and butchered here for centuries. Smithfield was once London's most notorious place to witness torture and executions.

Office workers hastily rush around, shopping at lunchtime in Cheapside. This has always been the busiest shopping street of the City. Saxone advertises its shoes for 16s 6d a pair, and a bus on its way 'up west' advertises Maples, the high-quality and fashionable furniture makers of Tottenham Court Road.

A view of Billingsgate dock from Custom House Quay. Steamers and other vessels arrive and depart carrying fresh fish to and from the market.

Billingsgate Christian Mission, St Mary-at-Hill, in 1914. The Mission was founded in 1878 to teach the gospel and provide spiritual help and medical treatment for Billingsgate workers, their families and people who lived and worked around the market. A doctor visited it regularly and there was a 10-bedded ward where patients could be nursed after minor surgery. Nurses are seen on the upper floor, surveying the busy scenes below. Regular services and Sunday school were also held there, and merchants from nearby Eastcheap often brought gifts for the children. As the years passed there was a diminishing need for the Mission and its doors finally closed in 1990.

(Pictured left): Busy Billingsgate Fish Market, Thames Street, in 1924. Many types of fish have been sold at Billingsgate since the 17th century, but not eels, which were sold by Dutch fishermen who moored in the Thames. Until the 19th century, fish was sold from Billingsgate dock. This arrangement was not satisfactory so the City's architect, Sir Horace Jones, built a special market, which opened in 1876. Billingsgate Market moved to modern premises in London Docklands in 1992.

Monument Street in 1946. Billingsgate workers hurry to and fro, and a horsedrawn cart, piled high with crates of fish, manoeuvres past a chatting police officer. The Monument, built to commemorate the Great Fire of London, towers in the background.

Commuters outside Moorgate Street Station, which belonged to the Metropolitan Railway Company. There were four stations within a few yards of each other that laid claim to the same name. Each was owned by an independent railway company, and they once all competed for passengers. They have now merged into one operating body, the London Underground.

A train stands by the platform at Moorgate Street Station in 1904. This platform belonged to the Great Northern and City Railway Company that ran tube trains from Finsbury Park, a distance of three and a half miles, into Moorgate.

Leadenhall Market, Whittington Avenue, takes its name from a house with a lead roof that stood here long ago. Above is the grand entrance to a market that is little changed, and below is the busy market with small shops, delivery vehicles and people going about their daily business, photographed in 1894. The hooks lining the shop exteriors are still there to remind us that a poultry market has been here since the Middle Ages. Leadenhall Market was the setting of Diagon Alley in the 2001 film *Harry Potter and the Philosopher's Stone (A)*

Throgmorton Street buzzing with stockbrokers and City businessmen. The sign on the right marked the entrance to the visitors gallery where visitors could watch the Stock Exchange at work. The Exchange moved to new hi-tech offices in Paternoster Square in 2004.

THE
STOCK EXCHANGE
VISITORS
GALLERY

The London Stock Exchange in the 1960s, where over 2,000 stockers, jobbers, members and clerks once worked on the trading floor before the 'Big Bang' in 1986.

At work in the Port of London. Lightermen, along with the watermen, were given the right to work on the river by Act of Parliament in 1555. One of the many tugboats that worked in the docks is visible in the background. Trade on the river has made an important contribution to the City's business since the Roman invasion 2,000 years ago.

The General Post Office in St Martin's-le-Grand in 1908. This is a typical working day with people going about their business. A large area around St Martin's-le-Grand was demolished in 1829 to make way for the new complex of buildings of the General Post Office headquarters. The Post Office used an assortment of vehicles to transport letters and parcels around the City. The City's main sorting office was in King Edward Street.

Parcel post was first introduced in 1883. This postcard, c.1905, shows a Post Office handcart that was used throughout London for deliveries in the Edwardian period. The deliverymen are wearing their fashionable uniforms, frock coats and shiny peaked caps. (A)

An early motorised tricycle used throughout the capital for Royal Mail deliveries. No registration marks on the vehicle and the cipher of Queen Victoria dates the photograph as pre-1902. *(A)*

An early motorised Royal Mail van, probably parked outside the City's main sorting office. Mail transport was subcontracted to outside delivery companies until after World War Two. The van pictured here belonged to McNamara Transport Company, whose depot was in Castle Street, Shoreditch. *(A)*

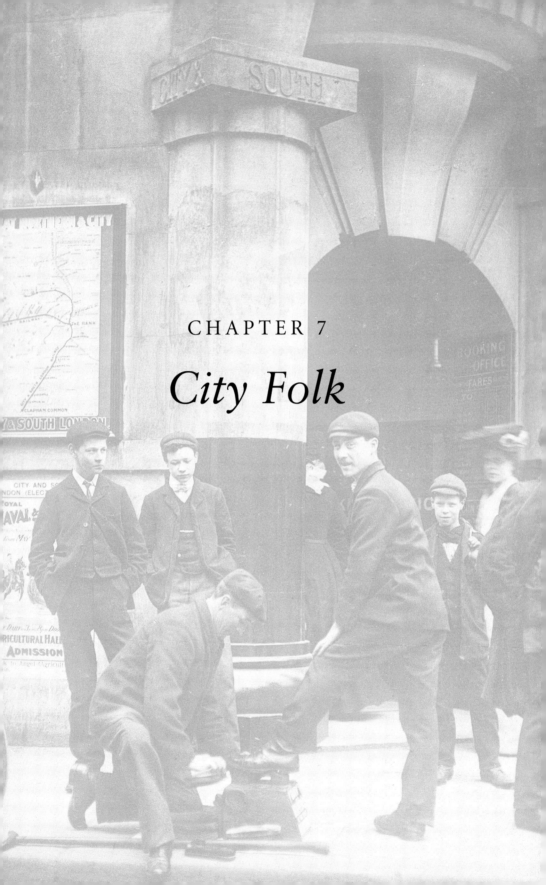

CHAPTER 7

City Folk

A horse-drawn, automatic road-sweeping vehicle seen around the warehouses of the City and close to the docks of London.

Office workers, visitors and their children feed the pigeons outside St Paul's Cathedral. This early picture shows that there were once plenty of pigeons in the City of London as well as in Trafalgar Square. The steps of St Paul's were featured in the 1964 hit musical film *Mary Poppins*.

A Royal Exchange
constable on the steps of
the Exchange in 1900.
These constables wore
blue and gold-braided
uniforms and they had the
authority to ensure that
the peace was kept within
the confines of the
Exchange. They also
had powers of arrest
and detention when
necessary. The last
remaining
constable retired
in 1980.

The District Messenger
Company provided reliable
boys as messengers in the
City. At a moment's notice
these boys could be asked to
deliver a letter, hail a cab,
hold a place in a queue or
run errands anywhere in
London.

Mr Edge, a fruit hawker, who
sold cherries and bananas, was a
popular figure often seen outside
Spiers and Pond department
store on Queen Victoria Street in
the 1930s. The notice on his
barrow reads: *To Motorists,
Athletes and others. S.F. Edge says
when racing, one of the chief
articles of diet is BANANAS which
are very sustaining.*

Selling hot chestnuts in Upper Thames Street in 1913. The brass licence-plate strapped to this street trader's arm identifies him as William George Davis, who was licensed to sell ice creams in the summer and hot chestnuts during the winter.

A bootblack boy busily shining the shoes of commuters emerging from King William Street Station on the City and South London Railway, now the Northern Line. This station and Bank Underground Station belonged to the Central Railway Company, now the Central Line. The two stations merged in 1933 when the London Passenger Transport Board was formed, which eventually became London Underground.

A cab rank in Lothbury, a street occupied by bankers and merchants. Hansom cabs were introduced on to London's streets in 1836. They were the fastest means of getting around the City until petrol-driven taxis were introduced in 1907. However, horse-drawn cabs were still to be seen in the late 1920s, the last one disappearing in 1947. The church in the background is St Margaret's, Lothbury.

Harry Cameron, 'The Great Carmo', brings 'Baby June', the elephant, and 'Punch', his teddy bear, on a day-trip to the City in the late 1920s. Mr Cameron, an illusionist and magician, often appeared on the West End stage with his menagerie of exotic animals. He is standing at the road junction of Princes Street and Gresham Street, with the Bank of England's Tivoli Corner in the background.

A costermonger, probably around Houndsditch, with sacks of second-hand clothes in his cart on the way to market in Petticoat Lane. This peddler must have been wealthy as he owns a horse, not a donkey. They would sometimes accept crockery and household goods as an alternative to cash.

Fruiterers abounded in most parts of the City, not least in Moorfields where these street traders sold their fruit outside the Moorfields branch of Boots the Cash Chemist. This was the 18th branch of Boots and was opened by Jesse Boot, the founder, in 1901.

The Central Meat Market in Smithfield. Butchers, wholesalers and meat porters take a moment from their duties to pose for this early photograph taken at the Market, the centre of the country's meat trade.

A Smithfield Bummaree or meat porter. Butchers who bought their meat at Smithfield engaged the services of the self-employed Bummarees to carry meat or poultry out to waiting vans and lorries.

A peddler displaying his wares in the City streets. Like the stockbrokers, bankers and solicitors he, too, proudly wears his bowler hat, the true badge of a City businessman.

In the postcard on the right, Polly the parrot greets Princess Mary, daughter of King George V, and the Lord Mayor, outside Ye Olde Cheshire Cheese in Wine Office Court in 1919. Polly, who was unusually foul-mouthed, was a gift to the landlord by an old sailor who used to drink at the Cheese. She became a favourite with customers and used to entertain royalty and visitors from all over the world. On Armistice night in 1918 Polly fainted after imitating the popping and glugging of champagne bottles over 400 times. When she died in 1926, at the ripe old age of 40, the news of her death was broadcast all over the world by the BBC, and over 200 obituaries were published in newspapers worldwide. Polly can still be seen in this famous inn, but she is now stuffed and on display in a cage as can be seen in the postcard above.

Entitled 'The happy carrier', this photograph, taken in 1939, shows a Billingsgate porter balancing crates of fresh kippers on his 'bobbin hat'. These flat-topped hats were traditionally worn by porters in this market, together with their white sailcloth smocks. *(D)*

101

Street vendors displaying their trinkets, newspapers and City street maps on Ludgate Hill in the early 1900s.

A ceremonial turn-out at Cannon Street Fire Station, c.1915. A new motorised fire appliance, on the far right, stands alongside two older horse-drawn appliances. Horses were employed to pull long-ladders before they were finally phased out in the 1920s.

The coach driver of Sir William Treloar perched high above the crowds waiting for the off. The message on the reverse of this postcard reads: *This is the chap that Lord Mayor Treloar took over to Paris with the coach and horses. The Lord Mayor stated that it was not the carriage, horses or himself that interested the French, but it is the coachman who is very stout.*

Lord Mayor Sir William Treloar in the year of his Mayoralty, 1906–7. Sir William founded the Treloar Trust with the intention of relieving the appalling plight of London's crippled children. With the charitable moneys raised during his year of office, he established the Lord Mayor Treloar Cripples Home and College at Alton, Hampshire. Today the principal purpose of the Trust is to provide a first-class education for young people with disabilities and has maintained close links with the City of London since its foundation.

All main thoroughfares in the City were hosed down and cleaned each night. At about 2am hoses were fitted to the hydrants and men dressed in oilskin aprons washed the day's filth into the gutters. Billingsgate fishmarket, where this photograph was taken, was notoriously unsavoury for its fishy smells and waste.

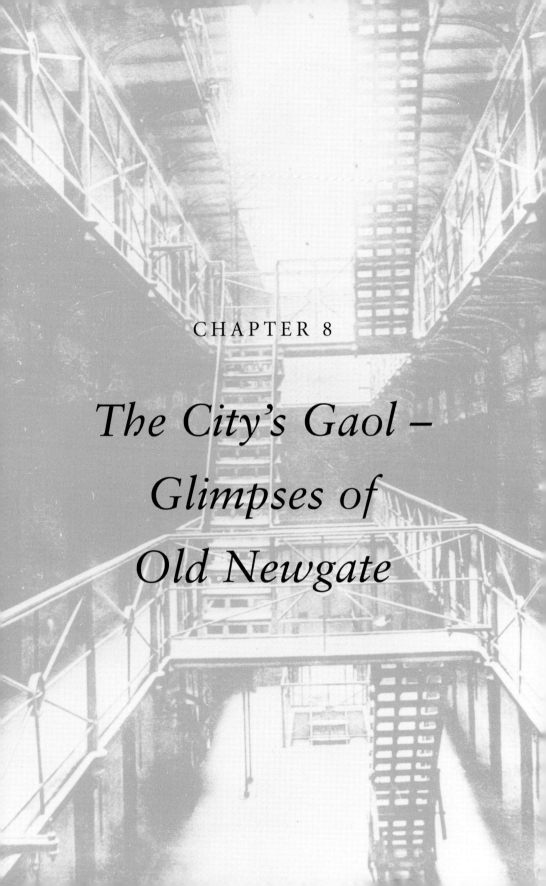

CHAPTER 8

The City's Gaol – Glimpses of Old Newgate

Newgate Prison had the reputation of being the most notorious penal institution in England. Throughout its long and often turbulent history some of the most dangerous criminals in England were imprisoned here. Eighteenth-century prison reformers John Howard and Elizabeth Fry desperately tried to alleviate the plight of the appalling conditions endured by prisoners.

However, in 1902, the prison was finally emptied out and torn down to make way for the new Central Criminal Court, The Old Bailey. The remains of dead prisoners were exhumed and reburied with Christian dignity in the City of London Cemetery in East London.

These rare photographs and postcards give a glimpse of Old Newgate before its demolition.

A simple lock-up in a room above one of the old gates was the original prison in the 12th century. Designed to confine petty criminals, curfew breakers and vagabonds, the acquisition of adjacent buildings and land in the 15th century meant that the prison could be rebuilt and enlarged to accommodate more prisoners.

A simple plaque embedded into the wall of the Central Criminal Court is a reminder that the gate, also called Newgate, was demolished in 1777. Most of the city's gates were pulled down by then to ease the flow of ever increasing traffic into the City.

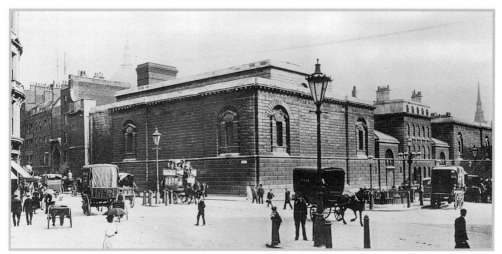

Newgate Gaol in 1900. This massive, dark and gloomy prison was rebuilt after riots in 1780 and became the most notorious and squalid penal institution in the country. When public hangings ceased at Tyburn (Marble Arch) in 1783, the open space in the foreground of the prison, known as Old Bailey, became London's principal execution site, where thousands of people came to enjoy the spectacle of public hangings. Outside people are going about their daily lives, probably unaware of the over-crowdedness, squalor and misery behind the foreboding walls.

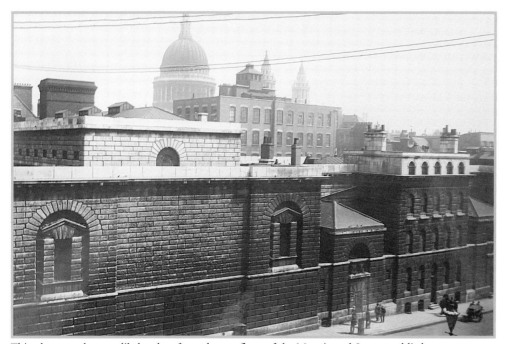

This photograph, most likely taken from the top floor of the Magpie and Stump public house across the road, looks over the roofs of the prison to St Paul's Cathedral a short distance away. The Magpie and Stump became a popular venue before public executions were abolished. The publican would hire out the upper rooms and a window seat overlooking the gallows, could cost up to £10, then a vast fortune.

Surprisingly, the main entrance to the prison was a small, solitary door set into the heavy walls. The scaffold and gallows used for public executions was erected to its left. The shackles and chains above the entrance are a solemn reminder of what lay within. *(A)*

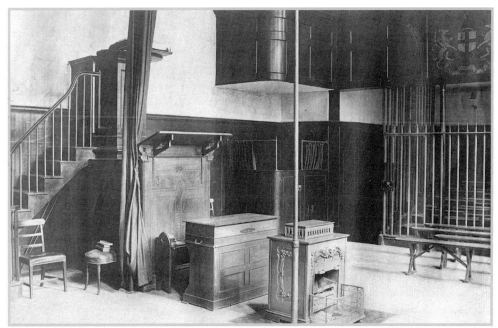

The interior of Newgate chapel. In front of the steps to the pulpit is the chair on which the condemned prisoner sat during their last service on the Sunday before 'Execution Monday'. Their coffin was placed on the chapel table during the service, but this practice was abandoned in 1817. The Governor's pew is seen below the pulpit.

The old courtroom of the Sessions House in Old Bailey, adjoining the prison, on the site of the Surgeons' Hall. Prisoners would be taken from their cells directly into the courtroom on 'Trial Fridays', with executions three days later on 'Execution Mondays'. From 1752 to 1809, the bodies of executed criminals were taken to Surgeons' Hall for dissection. They were publicly anatomised in the theatre, often before a large audience. Dissection was abolished in 1834.

Prison warders await an intake of new arrivals to be detained before their trials. The prison eventually became a holding prison for those to be tried at the Sessions House next door. *(A)*

The dimly lit and foreboding galleries of Newgate. The iron staircases lead to the walkways and cells of this massive prison.

Mrs Fry's Gate and the exercise yard for women prisoners. This gate was named after Elizabeth Fry, prison reformer and Quaker, who, at the beginning of the 19th century, befriended female prisoners in Newgate. She was so shocked at the filth and degradation endured by women and their small children while incarcerated that she formed 'the Association for the Improvement of the Females at Newgate'. Mrs Fry spent her life working to improve the conditions for women prisoners throughout the country.

This long, narrow courtyard was the 'exercising ground' for condemned men, and the barred windows on the left are the cells of murderers. They reached the yard through the door set into the wall between the windows.

The interior of one of the cells. Its dimensions measured 7ft wide, 13ft long and 8ft 10 inches high. The walls were whitewashed and each cell contained simple wooden furnishings and a gas lamp fitted on to the wall above the desk. The three framed prints are simple messages declaring God's love for man.

Deadmen's Walk, where executed felons were buried below the paving slabs of the passageway that led from the Old Bailey Sessions House to the prison. On their return from trial, the condemned prisoners knew that they were walking over the ground that was to be their own graves. A warden and prison official, attracted by the camera, are standing on these flagstones. *(A)*

The chief warden stands with his back to the condemned cell holding his bunch of keys. Out of sight is the dreaded execution shed which came into use in 1868, the year public executions in England were abolished. *(A)*

The last man to be publicly hanged in Great Britain was Michael Barrett, a Fenian terrorist who supported Irish nationalism. He was executed outside Newgate in 1868 before a large crowd. After that, executions were carried out privately in the shed on the right of the exercise yard. Only invited guests, such as reporters and dignitaries, were allowed to attend.

A rare view of the interior of the execution shed showing the scaffold. The condemned prisoner stood on the closed trapdoor with a noose around his neck and wearing a white hood. The rope was attached to the chain in the centre of the beam, and upon a signal the trap would drop open and the prisoner would drop into the pit below. A doctor would then certify that the prisoner was dead. Between 1868 and 1902, 58 men and five women were hanged here. The shed was demolished in 1902 shortly before the prison closed down and the scaffold was removed to Pentonville Prison in North London.

At midnight, on the eve of executions, the bellman of St Sepulchre's Church, opposite the prison, stood in front of the window of the condemned prisoners' cell and recited the following verse while loudly ringing the bell that is on display there:

All you that in the condemned hole do lie,
Prepare you, for tomorrow you shall die;
Watch all, and pray; the hour is drawing near,
That you before the Almighty must appear.
Examine well yourselves; in time repent,
That you may not to eternal flames be sent,
And when St Sepulchre's Bell in the morning tolls,
The Lord have mercy on your souls.

Whipping post and shackles. These gruesome instruments of punishment lie abandoned in the once overcrowded gaol. Newgate was designed to hold 4,027 prisoners. On one occasion more than 8,000 were huddled together in severely overcrowded conditions creating gaol fever and other infectious diseases. The prisoners were not provided with bedding, and the rations were hardly sufficient to sustain life. Inmates relied heavily on food being brought in by their families or friends. Warders were often 'on the make', selling food at vastly inflated prices. *(A)*

This studded black door, made in 1709, used to be the Debtors' door. When the prison closed, visitors flocked to purchase mementoes including furniture. The door is now an entrance to a private residence in north-west London.

Looking north towards Newgate Street. Prison vans entered through this double set of gates to offload detainees awaiting trial at the Old Bailey Sessions House.

A simple stone plaque marks the site of the mass grave of prisoners. Their bodies were removed from Newgate during demolition and reburied in the City of London Cemetery, East London.

Eighty-one temporary cells were put up before demolition work began on the prison in 1902. They were to hold prisoners awaiting trial in the Sessions House next door. A company called The Fireproof Partition Syndicate Ltd, specialising in temporary buildings, was contracted to erect them from corrugated steel sheeting strong enough to resist any escape. This was the first time pre-fabricated buildings of any kind were used. They were the prototype for thousands of homes to be built in the new colonies of South Africa. The two photographs show the hoarding erected by the company and the temporary cells during construction outside the prison walls.

Tall gantry cranes had been erected after completion of the demolition in 1903. For a short time there was an uninterrupted view of St Paul's from the corner of Giltspur Street and Newgate Street. *(H)*

The Central Criminal Court, the nation's most famous courthouse, was built on the site of the prison. The original Sessions House was much too small with only four courtrooms and 90 cells for prisoners brought for trial. This is the new building, designed by architect Edward Mountford in the grand, European style, which cost nearly £400,000.

The grand opening ceremony held on 27 February 1907 in the presence of King Edward VII and Queen Alexandra.

The Grand Entrance to the 1907 building in Old Bailey. The statues over the entrance, sculpted by Frederick William Pomeroy, depicts the Recording Angel with Fortitude and Truth on either side. Above them Pomeroy carved the inscription: *Defend the children of the poor and punish the wrongdoer*, a verse from Psalm 72.

The figure of Justice stands high above the City streets. In one hand she holds the scales of justice and in the other, the sword of retribution. Unlike other statues of justice, she is not blindfolded as she is overseeing justice being done. Among those who were tried at the Old Bailey were: Oscar Wilde for sodomy in 1895, on his release from prison, Wilde lived in Paris where he died in 1900; Serial killer Timothy Evans for the 10 Rillington Place murders, hanged in 1953; Dr Hawley Harvey Crippen, who was the first man to be identified through the use of telegraphy, hanged for murdering his wife in 1910; Ruth Ellis who killed her lover and was the last woman to be hanged in England in 1955 and the infamous 1960s gangster twins, Reggie and Ronnie Kray. *(A)*

CHAPTER 9

City Police,
Law and Order

The City of London Police Force was established in 1839 by an Act of Parliament. This new force of 500 men had no legal jurisdiction beyond the City boundaries until restrictions were lifted in the early 1950s. Unlike all other police forces, the City police are responsible to the Corporation of London and not the Home Secretary in Westminster.

By 1910 the Force had reached its peak strength of more than 1,800 men within the City. Women, however, were not recruited until 1949. Today the force is separated into two territorial divisions operating out of Bishopsgate and Snow Hill police stations. Its operational headquarters is in Wood Street. Today there over 1,200 people employed by the Force.

Fraudulent allegations, at home or abroad, involving the City financial markets will normally result in the City Police being involved. Therefore, they have justification for having the most effective fraud squad in the world. Their success rate in all other areas of crime is the envy of most other forces.

Frank Francis joined the City of London Police Force in 1880. On enrolling as a constable, his yearly salary was 93s. (£4.80). He rose through the ranks and was appointed Chief Clerk and Senior Superintendent before he finally retired in 1909 on a salary of £297 a year. He was one of only five officers in the Force to be awarded the King Edward VII Coronation Medal, in 1902.

Sergeants William Whacker, on the left, and Edwin Sharplin. These officers enlisted in 1868 and 1877 respectively. This austere portrait photograph dates from the 1890s. The styles of uniforms have changed dramatically between these two officers and Superintendent Francis in the previous photograph.

Officers of the City of London Police Force with their Chief Inspector in 1907. It is thought that this photograph was taken at Guildhall as part of the Lord Mayor's Day celebrations.

A group of senior officers and constables of the 4th Division based at Cloak Lane police station in 1910. Cloak Lane station, near Cheapside, closed in 1965. Those who were employed there were transferred to other locations.

A sergeant of the mounted branch of the City Police, *c.*1920. Police horses were kept at the Whitbread Brewery stables alongside the big shire horses that pulled the beer wagons. The horses were later housed with the Lord Mayor's coach until purpose built stables were established at Wood Street Police Office in 1964.

A policeman on traffic duty at a busy City road junction. This postcard, entitled 'The Arm of the Law', was hastily withdrawn due to the flagrant advertising of an alcoholic beverage. It is interesting to note the diversity of transport in the scene. *(C)* (*©Judges Postcards Ltd, Hastings*)

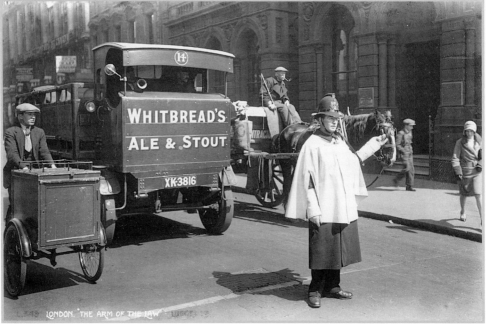

In 1903 City policemen took some 1,705 people to hospital, half of them strapped to one of the Force's wheeled hand-litters. In 1907 the first ambulances, powered by electricity, were purchased and an ambulance service, staffed and supervised by the force, was brought into operation. This was the forerunner of other ambulance services in the British Isles.

A female member of the Auxiliary Police Corp serving with the City Police in 1944. This smartly dressed young woman is standing next to a City police ambulance. In 1949 the City of London's own police ambulance service was integrated into the London Ambulance Service.

This unusual postcard entitled 'May Good Luck Cross your Path' shows a caring officer on traffic duty seeing a black cat across the busy street. The crest of his helmet with its Roman-style comb reminds us that as the Romans protected the City 2,000 years ago, the City of London Police protect it today.

Each night policemen patrolled every street, alleyway and courtyard in the Square Mile. They even went so far as to climb up ladders to check that warehouse windows were tightly and safely secured, c.1910.

Motorised prison vans were introduced into the City Police Force in 1921. This example is a converted lorry once used for delivering goods around the capital. It was converted to a 'Black Maria' later. The name 'Black Maria' is said to have come from a large and powerful black woman named Maria Lee who helped constables in Boston, Massachusetts, to escort drunks to the cells in the 1830s. The name became the popular nickname for police vehicles.

Although body-snatchers and resurrectionists disappeared at the beginning of the 19th century, City policemen were still carrying out night duty in churchyards in 1910.

These two postcards were published in the 1920s. The photographs were taken near Mansion House (above) and the Royal Exchange (below). They are part of a series entitled 'Safety First'. The captions on the reverse read: '*The control of the traffic by the London Policeman is the constant theme of warm approval from visitors hailing from all over the world. His courtesy and kindness to the aged wayfarer, the stranger or the inexperienced, dazed by the turmoil and traffic of our streets, is equally worthy of a word of praise.*'

Sidney Street Siege

On the night of 16 December 1910, three unarmed City policemen were killed and two seriously injured attempting to arrest a gang of Latvian burglars who were tunneling into a jeweller's shop from an adjoining building in the Exchange Buildings, Houndsditch. Their leader was a mysterious character nicknamed 'Peter the Painter' and their motive was to fund a revolution in Latvia. For two of the gang, their end came two weeks later in the famous Siege of Sidney Street.

The wording on the memorial dedicated to Sergeants Tucker and Bentley buried at the City of London Cemetery in Manor Park, East London reads:

'In appreciation of their devotion to duty this monument is erected by the Police Committee and by the Officers and Constables of the City of London Police Force'.

This memorial card was published in memory of the three City policemen, Sergeants Robert Bentley and Charles Tucker and Constable Joseph Choate.

Following a state funeral for all three brave officers at St Paul's Cathedral, Sergeants Bentley and Tucker were interred on 22 December 1910 at the City of London Cemetery in Manor Park, East London. PC Choate was buried at Byfleet Cemetery in Surrey. The three were posthumously awarded the King's Police Medal. Eight Latvian anarchists were later arrested for their part in the murders. Two of the gang were discovered at 100 Sidney Street in London's East End, approximately two miles from the incident.

On 3 January 1911 City of London Police and Metropolitan Police wait patiently in Sidney Street after two of the anarchists barricaded themselves into a house. Mr Winston Churchill, the Home Secretary, summoned an armed battalion of Scots Guards from the Tower of London. Amazingly, everyday life went on as normal nearby and a postman actually made his rounds a few houses away.

Mr Winston Churchill, wearing top hat and cloak, takes charge and observes the battle from the heart of the fire zone.

Six hours later a fire began to consume the building. When no more return shots were heard the fire brigade set to work extinguishing the fire. Inside the remains of two members of the gang were recovered having choked to death. 'Peter the Painter' was never found.

Supt. Lucas, standing on the right with a colleague, outside the sand-bagged Snow Hill Police Station in 1939 at the start of World War Two. Wearing their tin helmets, these eager police officers are seen waiting to repel an invasion that never happened.

A close-up of Supt. Lucas peeping from behind his well-entrenched fortress at Snow Hill.

136

A friendly police officer points the way during the thick London smog of the 1950s. Many of the City's monuments and famous buildings were thickly covered by black soot and grime, and thousands of Londoners died of respiratory illnesses. The Clean Air Act was passed in 1956, and eventually London's air became bearable and the buildings cleaner.

A police officer on traffic duty shortly before manually-controlled traffic lights were introduced in 1930. Two years later the first automatic traffic lights in Europe were installed in the City. This photograph was taken at the junction of Fleet Street and Ludgate Circus. *(C)* (*©Judges Postcards Ltd, Hastings*)

On traffic duty at Bank Junction in 1906.

CHAPTER 10

The City at War

*'We would rather see London laid in ruins and ashes
than that it should be tamely and adjectively enslaved'.*

Mr Winston Churchill, Prime Minister.

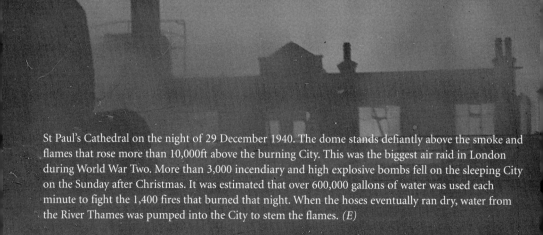

St Paul's Cathedral on the night of 29 December 1940. The dome stands defiantly above the smoke and flames that rose more than 10,000ft above the burning City. This was the biggest air raid in London during World War Two. More than 3,000 incendiary and high explosive bombs fell on the sleeping City on the Sunday after Christmas. It was estimated that over 600,000 gallons of water was used each minute to fight the 1,400 fires that burned that night. When the hoses eventually ran dry, water from the River Thames was pumped into the City to stem the flames. *(E)*

Further damage in Fore Street. At the end of hostilities, large areas of the City were laid to waste as illustrated in this contemporary postcard, photographed in 1945.

Civil Defence personnel methodically search for missing people in the debris of buildings ripped apart.

Sunday 25 August 1940 was like every other quiet weekend day until all hell broke loose when bombs began to reign down on an unsuspecting City. The first fell in Fore Street at 12.15am. Charred and burnt-out buildings include the offices of the Greengate and Irwell Rubber Company and Westminster Bank who shared No.12 Fore Street, the white building to the right of the photograph. Next door Chappell Allen, the corset maker, and Pinter and Company, wax figure makers, moved elsewhere to more secure premises. It was estimated that more than 40 high explosive and incendiary bombs fell within the first four minutes, crippling water and gas mains. This photograph shows the extent of the damage. It was taken as dawn broke to reveal the full extent of the horror. No one could imagine the destruction that lay ahead. *(B)*

The deep hole created by a 2,000kg unexploded high-explosive bomb that fell close to the south-west tower of St Paul's Cathedral during a raid on 12 December 1940. It buried itself deep below the pavement, threatening the tower's foundations. Sapper George Wylie of the Bomb Disposal Section of the Royal Engineers was responsible for its safe removal. Wylie and his team worked for three days in dangerous and uncomfortable conditions. The fear that the bomb would explode was made worse by fractured and burning gas mains. After they finally succeeded to prise the bomb from the deep pit, they drove it to Hackney Marshes in East London where it was destroyed in a controlled explosion. The 100ft crater testified to the damage St Paul's would have suffered had the bomb gone off. George Wylie was awarded the George Cross for his courage and skill. *(B)*

Office workers stand outside a branch of Lloyds Bank in King Arthur Street, probably discussing the air-raids of the previous night. Both high explosive and incendiary bombs were deployed here in early September 1940. *(B)*

A closer view of the No.5 London Transport bus in the above photograph. A fire officer surveys the extensive damage. This bus was on its way into the City from Wimbledon in south London. London's buses became a symbol of survival and resistance, operating throughout the metropolitan area whatever the conditions. *(B)*

St Paul's Cathedral suffered two direct hits with incendiary bombs. One punched a hole in the roof and fell into the nave at the east end. Daylight shines down onto the damaged Victorian high altar. Lying among the rubble, on the right of the picture below, is the Dean's Sedilia. The much beloved Jewelled Cross was found broken among the debris. *(B)*

The second bomb fell through the roof of the North Transept into the crypt below, making a large hole in the floor of the nave. The Cathedral's Treasury now occupies the crypt area where the bomb fell. These photographs show the devastation caused. *(B)*

The City's tallest steeple, 221ft 9in, belonging to Sir Christopher Wren's St Mary le Bow Church, stands tall above the ruins of Cheapside. The famous 'Cockney' church was gutted on the night of 29 December 1940 leaving only the tower and steeple intact. The photograph was taken looking east over Bread Street. *(inset)* The inset shows the charred and burnt out interior open to the sky. *(B)*

A burnt-out train belonging to the Metropolitan Railway Company stands on the track leading into Moorgate Station. This view was photographed from Moor Lane Bridge at the station's rear. *(B)*

Moorgate Station on 29 December 1940. St Paul's dome is clearly visible in the distance. The buildings in Aldermanbury and Basinghall Street are seen through the blackened arch, all that remains of a burnt-out train shed.

Foliage almost hides a stretch of the mediaeval City wall in St Alphege Gardens. This defensive wall was built above the Roman original. It once stood adjacent to St Alphege Church, demolished in 1923. The tower of the ancient Church of St Giles Without Cripplegate peeps out above the trees.

Inside the nave of St Giles Without Cripplegate. It was here that William Shakespeare worshipped, Oliver Cromwell married and John Milton, author of *Paradise Lost,* was buried. It is an open shell after the destruction of 29 and 30 December 1940.

The lone tower of St Giles Without Cripplegate stands proud among the ruins. A bus trundles through London Wall, following the line where the Roman Wall of London once stood, in utter desolation. The origin of the word Cripplegate could be from the Anglo-Saxon word 'crepel', meaning a covered way leading to a gate of a mediaeval walled city. An alternative origin is that cripples and beggars sheltered here, under the covered way.

An unexploded parachute mine with its casing shattered lies at the edge of a footway, its deadly cargo of explosive material littering the roadside. The fuses had already been removed when this photograph was taken after a bombing raid on 16 October 1940. The size of this mine was 8ft 6in long by 2ft 9in diameter. *(B)*

The remains of St Olave's, Hart Street, the damage caused by a high explosive bomb on 17 April 1941. This mediaeval church was built in 1450 and survived London's Great Fire of 1666. St Olave's was rebuilt after the war. Samuel Pepys, the celebrated 17th century diarist, is buried here with his wife. *(B)*

Guildhall is the ancient seat of City Government. The Great Hall, built in 1411, is seen here after an air raid. Monuments to our nation's heroes Lord Nelson and the Duke of Wellington are damaged and charred, and timbers from the roof and debris lie scattered about. This hall was the scene of major trials and great ceremonial events. Among those condemned to death here were Lady Jane Grey, queen for nine days, Henry Garnet, a gunpowder plot conspirator of 1605, and Dr Rodrigo Lopez, royal physician to Elizabeth I. Dr Lopez was wrongly accused of an attempt on the Queen's life and executed. The Great Hall, one of the finest mediaeval halls in England, was restored in 1954. *(B)*

The steeple and tower of Greyfriars' Church in Newgate Street. Wren's famous church was rebuilt after the Great Fire of London only to be destroyed for a second time in the inferno of the Blitz. The headquarters of the General Post Office is in the background. A memorial garden now replaces the church but the steeple and tower still stand. The low, white building to the right of the truck was the entrance to St Paul's Underground Station. It is probable that this postcard was printed at the end of the hostilities in 1945 because cranes are clearly visible in the background.

A young boy stands with his back to the camera, staring into the distance. This ancient street, Aldermanbury, was where the Aldermen (elders) of the City of London lived many hundreds of years ago.

Vegetation grows where buildings once stood in Bridgewater Square, in the Barbican. A branch of Barclays Bank, on the corner of Golden Lane, has been badly damaged. Note the allotments with vegetation growing on the bomb sites in the foreground.

No. 23 Queen Victoria Street collapses in flames on Sunday 11 May 1941. The ground floor offices and showroom were occupied by a company of cigar importers and the offices above by firms of accountants and solicitors. The Luftwaffe were instructed not to return to their bases in northern France until their bomb bays were emptied. The low tide of the Thames that night made it even more difficult for the firefighters to pump river water into the City to put out the flames when other sources ran dry. *(B)*

Looking west down Ludgate Hill. Beyond the railway bridge, now gone, is Ludgate Circus and Fleet Street. The wedding cake steeple of St Bride's Church towers over the burnt-out shells of buildings, the damage being sustained on 10 and 11 May 1941.

A large section of The Central
Criminal Court, famously
known throughout the world
as the Old Bailey, was
destroyed in the bombing raid
of 10 May 1941.

When dawn broke on the morning of 12 September 1941, the full horror of the previous night's bombing became apparent. A direct hit to the main thoroughfare at Bank Junction caused a high-explosive bomb to penetrate into the Central Line booking hall of Bank Underground Station. This photograph shows the havoc it caused. The Royal Exchange bears the wartime slogan *Dig for Victory*, and the Bank of England is to the left. *(B)*

The 120ft wide bomb crater, London's largest, is clearly visible in the foreground. The main casualties, in excess of 130 killed or wounded, were City workers sheltering on the escalators and platforms at the time of the explosion. Several people were blown onto the tracks as a train pulled into the station. Other injuries and fatalities were caused by collapsing ceilings and flying glass from the windows of the train. With no way to the surface, survivors walked in semi-darkness along the Central Line tracks to emerge at the next station at Liverpool Street three hours later. Princes Street and the 18th-century protective walls of the Bank of England are in the background of this dramatic photograph. *(B)*

A No.15 bus, on its journey to Plaistow in East London, is crossing a temporary road bridge above the booking hall of the station. The men of the Pioneer Corps took seven days to clear away the debris. A further seven days were spent building the bridge by soldiers belonging to the Regiment of the Royal Engineers. Behind the bus is Mansion House. (B)

'At all costs, St Paul's Cathedral must be saved' were the words of Prime Minister Mr Winston Churchill that were heard by the nation at the start of hostilities over London. This is an aerial view of London's Cathedral majestically standing amid the shells and ruins of City offices, institutions and bombed churches. The open expanse to the left was Paternoster Square where, for many hundreds of years, booksellers, printers and bookbinders lived and worked together. To the far right, the tower of St Augustine's Church stands isolated apart from one other building on the corner of Old Change. St Paul's was saved by its own fire team, the St Paul's Fire Watch, volunteers from all walks of life. These brave men and women took turns on the roof to quickly extinguish the fires of incendiary bombs before they could cause even more severe damage.

London's Cathedral is illuminated by floodlights on VE (Victory in Europe) Day on 8 May 1945. Celebrations, singing and dancing and street parties took place all over London and throughout the country. At midnight Big Ben tolled to announce the official ceasefire. Mr Winston Churchill, broadcasting earlier in the day, said *'the war with Germany is at an end'.* He continued *'this is your victory'.*

This sculpture named 'Blitz' is the national memorial that honours the memories of more than 1,027 firefighters, both men and women, who gave their lives while defending the nation during World War Two. It was unveiled by HM Queen Elizabeth the Queen Mother in 1991. Prime Minister Mr Winston Churchill called the brave and fearless firefighters the 'Heroes with Grimy Faces'. Carved into the triangular pediment high above St Paul's is a phoenix, the mythical bird that burned itself to death and arose rejuvenated from its own ashes. This was Sir Christopher Wren's reminder of the Cathedral's rebirth after the Great Fire of 1666

Six years after the ending of World War Two King George V1 and the royal family greet the people of London from the steps of St Paul's Cathedral and declare the Festival of Britain open on 3 May 1951. The aim of the festival was to dispel the gloom caused by the war. There were parties in the streets, and funfairs and exhibitions were held all over Britain.

CHAPTER 11

The City of Fred Judge

This chapter is dedicated to the memory of
Fred Judge, 'The Postcard Man',
who did so much to help develop the
British picture postcard

Fred Judge was born in 1872, and at the age of twenty-three he developed a keen interest in photography.

At the turn of the twentieth century he settled in Hastings where he and his wife bought a photographic business. He often rose early to take local photographs, the quality of which were far superior to any postcard yet produced.

They lived over the shop that became the factory for the first Judges' postcards, but in 1910 they bought larger premises to provide greater production facilities. Ten years later Fred built a new factory where his postcards were produced by automatic process.

The first cards sold for 1d, but as costs increased so did his prices, until in 1968 monochrome postcards lost their popularity in favour of the high-quality coloured ones produced by the company that still bears his name.

Fred died, in 1951, at the age or 79 years having taken over 35,000 photographs that resulted in the mass-production of many millions of postcards bearing the name "Judges' of Hastings".

The postcards I have chosen for this chapter are from a series of over 800 views of London. My selection are early photographs of The Square Mile seen through the camera lens of Fred Judge, 'The Postcard Man'.

(© The Following images are the copyright of Judges Postcards Ltd. Other Judges postcards can be seen on pages 41, 68, 128 and 140).

The ancient gateway to the Church of St Bartholomew-the-Great in West Smithfield. The 16th century half-timbered gatehouse can been seen above the arched entrance. Could the gentleman in the photograph be Fred Judge? (C)

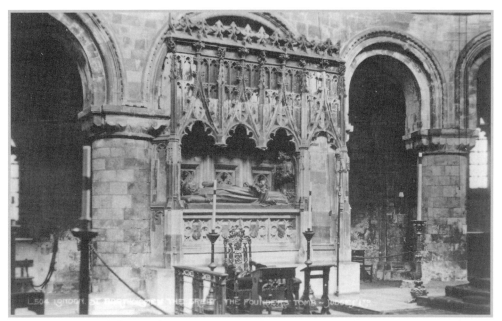

Above: Inside St Bartholomew-the-Great.
The tomb of Rahere, the founder, who was
buried beside the alter in 1143. (C)

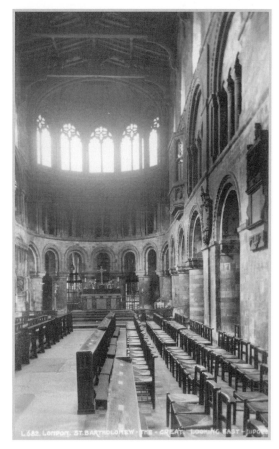

Inside St Bartholomew. This medieval
church was heavily restored in 1863, but still
retains most of its Norman and early
English Gothic features. (C)

167

Looking towards Smithfield from St Bartholomew's Hospital. To the right of the 18th century gateway is St Bartholomew-the-Less, the hospital's own parish church. (C)

The blurred figure of a nurse can be seen rushing about her duties of the quadrangle of St Barts. Is this really a nurse? Or did the eye of Fred Judge's camera capture the ghostly figure of the 'grey lady' who is said to haunt this hospital. (C)

Statue of 'Peace' serenely poised with hand outstretched in the garden in Smithfield. This place was once London's most notorious execution site. Here in 1305 the Scottish patriot Sir William Wallace, Braveheart, was hanged, drawn and quartered. Many hundreds of people were martyred here in the 16th century. (C)

All that remains of the parish church of St Alphage is a garden that once covered its graveyard, and a segment of London's defensive wall built by the Romans over 2000 years ago. (C)

The Roman bastion in St Giles' Churchyard, Cripplegate, situated in the 1960s built Barbican development. This tower was part of the Roman fortress that occupied the north-west corner of Roman London. (C)

A fairy-tale palace decked with turrets and towers –
in reality the Royal Courts of Justice seen from Fleet Street.
The lone figure staring towards the Temple Bar memorial could
be Fred Judge, or possibly his friend Norman Button, a photographer
and employee. (C)

Pilgrim Street was used as a shortcut to St Paul's from the, now vanished, River Fleet. This quaint and narrow street, with its small shops and horsedrawn vehicles, was typical of the City during the early years of the 20th century. (C)

A picturesque view of the White Tower, the oldest part of the Tower of London seen from Tower Bridge in 1913. The Tower, which stands outside the City's boundary, has often been described as the world's most famous castle. (C)

Trinity Square, circa 1912. A heavily laden horse and cart takes a breather on Tower Hill, close to the place where Lord Lovat, the last man to be beheaded in England was executed in 1747. The Tower of London and Tower Bridge are a suitable backdrop to this dramatic photograph. (C)

A pre-war view of St Mary-le-Bow church in Cheapside. Wren's grandest steeple, home of the famous Bow Bells, is crowned by a weather-vane designed as a giant dragon. It is so high up that passers-by rarely see it. To be a true Cockney, you have to be born within the sounds of Bow Bells. (C)

The Port of London Authority, Tower Hill. This was, perhaps, the finest example of Edwardian architecture built in the City of London, but was heavily criticised as too extravagant in 1922, the year it was opened by Mr Lloyd George, then Prime Minister. At the time of revising this book permission has been granted to convert the building into a luxury hotel. (C)

In the early years of the 20th century London's docks were the world's busiest. This view shows what it was really like to be amongst the barges, cranes and ocean going ships. (C)

175

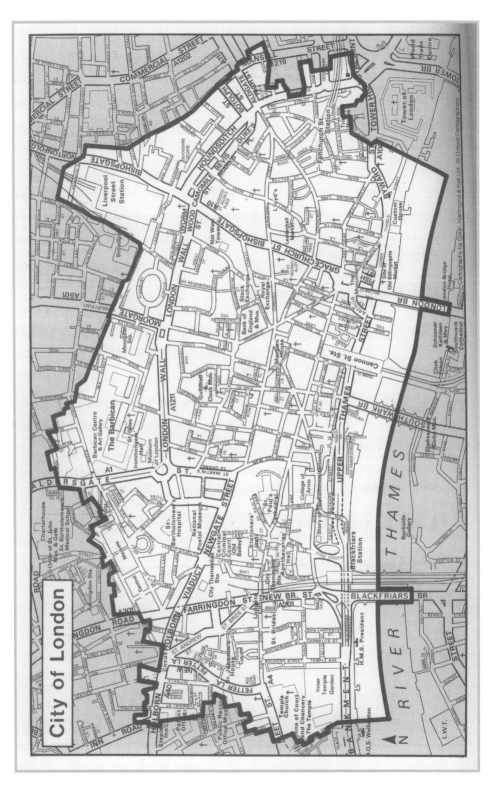

City of London